easy crochet
Country

30 projects to make for your home and to wear

Consultant: Nikki Trench

hamlyn

An Hachette UK Company
www.hachette.co.uk

First published in Great Britain in 2013 by
Hamlyn, a division of Octopus Publishing Group Ltd
Endeavour House
189 Shaftesbury Avenue
London
WC2H 8JY
www.octopusbooks.co.uk

ISBN 978-0-600-62833-0

A CIP catalogue record for this book is available from the
British Library

Printed and bound in China

10 9 8 7 6 5 4 3 2 1

Contents

Introduction

Crochet is easy, and it grows fast. Master a few basic stitches (and the terminology) and you can create stylish crocheted items to wear, use to decorate your home and as gifts for friends and family in next to no time and with minimal experience.

Whether you are a relative beginner, a confident convert or a long-term aficionado, there are projects here to delight. While your first attempts may be a bit uneven, a little practice and experimentation will ensure you soon improve. None of the projects in this book is beyond the scope of even those fairly new to the hobby. Even the most basic of stitches can be translated into covetable items.

Country style is perfect for crafts of all kinds and crochet is no exception. The projects in this book personify the charm and appeal of a bucolic existence – even if it is only in your dreams. Crochet gorgeous clothes, from wraps and scarves to cardigans and hats, or decorative and practical items for your country cottage such as throws and cushions.

Crochet essentials

All you really need to get crocheting is a hook and some yarn. For many projects that's it, and where additional items are required, most of these can be found in a fairly basic sewing kit. All measurements are given in metric and imperial. Choose which to work in and stick with it since conversions may not be exact in all instances.

- **Hooks** These are sized in mm (with 'old UK' sizes given as well) and can be made from wood, plastic, aluminium, bamboo or steel. The material affects the weight and 'feel' of the hook, and which you choose is largely down to personal preference.
- **Yarns** Specific yarns are given for each project, but if you want to make substitutions, full details of the yarn's composition and the ball lengths are given so that you can choose alternatives, either from the wide range of online sources, or from your local supplier, many of whom have very knowledgeable staff.

Do keep any leftover yarns (not forgetting the ball bands, since these contain vital information) to use for future projects.

- **Additional items** Some of the projects require making up and finishing, and need further materials and equipment, such as needles (both ordinary and round-pointed tapestry ones) and thread, buttons, ribbons and other accessories. These are detailed for each project in the Getting Started box.

What is in this book

All projects are illustrated with several photographs to show you the detail of the work – both inspirational and useful for reference. A full summary of each project is given in the Getting Started box so you can see exactly what's involved. Here, projects are graded from one star (straightforward, suitable for beginners) through two (more challenging) to three stars (for crocheters with more confidence and experience).

Also in the Getting Started box is the size of each finished item, yarn(s) and additional materials needed, and what tension the project is worked in. Finally, a breakdown of the steps involved is given so you know exactly what the project entails before you start.

At the start of the pattern instructions is a key to all abbreviations particular to the project and occasional notes expand if necessary.

Additional information

Occasionally, more information or a specialist technique is needed. How To boxes, diagrams and keys clarify these potentially tricky steps. The box on page 15, for example, explains how to work in the round for the Rustic Shopping Bag, while on page 68 a detailed diagram shows exactly how to lay out the squares for the Hexagonal Throw.

If you have enjoyed the projects here, you may want to explore the other titles in the Easy Crochet series: *Babies & Children*, *Flowers*, *Seaside*, *Vintage & Retro* and *Weekend*. For those who enjoy knitting, a sister series Easy Knitting, features similarly stylish yet simple projects.

Side-buttoning jacket

An easy stitch and luxurious yarn make this a delightful jacket to crochet and wear.

Worked in a solid stitch pattern and Aran yarn for warmth, this neat jacket has a military flavour especially with its stand-up collar and side-buttoned fastening.

GETTING STARTED

Simple patterned fabric but you will need to keep track of shaping.

Size:

To fit bust: *81–86[91–97:102–107]cm (32–34[36–38:40–42]in)*

Actual size: *92[102:112]cm (36[40:44]in)*

Length: *59[61:63]cm (23¼[24:24¾]in)*

Sleeve seam: *38cm (15in)*

Note: *Figures in square brackets [ ] refer to larger sizes; where there is only one set of figures, it applies to all sizes*

How much yarn:

7[8:9] x 100g (3½oz) hanks of Artesano Aran in Nightfall (shade 0807)

Hook:

5.50mm (UK 5) crochet hook

Additional items:

3 buttons
Stitch markers

Tension:

12 sts measure 10cm (4in) and 10 rows measure 10.5cm (4⅛in) over patt on 5.50mm (UK 5) hook
IT IS ESSENTIAL TO WORK TO THE STATED TENSION TO ACHIEVE SUCCESS

What you have to do:

Work pattern in alternating rows of double crochet and trebles. Work stitches together to shape side seams, armholes and neck. Make buttonholes in right front. Neaten front edges with double crochet.

The Yarn

Artesano Aran (approx. 132m/144 yards per 100g/3½oz ball) is a luxurious mixture of 50% alpaca and 50% wool. It is perfect for warm autumn/winter garments as the wool content keeps the yarn light so that larger items hold their shape. The colours are mainly subtle, with some bright contemporary shades as well.

Instructions

Abbreviations:

beg = beginning; **ch** = chain(s); **cm** = centimetre(s); **cont** = continue; **dc** = double crochet; **dc2tog** = work 1dc into each of next 2 sts leaving last loop of each on hook, yarn round hook and draw through all 3 loops; **dec** = decrease; **foll** = follow(s)(ing); **inc** = increase; **patt** = pattern; **rep** = repeat; **RS** = right side; **ss** = slip stitch; **st(s)** = stitch(es); **tog** = together; **tr** = treble(s); **tr2tog** = work 1tr into each of next 2 sts leaving last loop of each on hook, yarn round hook and draw through all 3 loops; **WS** = wrong side

BACK:

With 5.50mm (UK 5) hook make 56[62:68]ch.

Foundation row: (RS) 1dc into 2nd ch from hook, 1dc into each ch to end, turn. 55[61:67] sts.

* Next row: 1ch (does not count as a st), 1dc into each dc to end, turn.

Cont in patt as foll:

1st row: (RS) 3ch (counts as first tr), miss first dc, 1tr into each dc to end, turn.

2nd row: 1ch (does not count as a st), CrochetWeekend 1dc into each tr to end, working last dc into 3rd of 3ch, turn. Patt 3 more rows, ending with a RS row.*

Shape side seams:

Next row: (WS) 1ch, dc2tog over first 2tr, 1dc into each tr to last 2 sts, dc2tog over next tr and 3rd of 3ch, turn. 53[59:65] sts.

Work 1 row. Rep last 2 rows 3 times more. 47[53:59] sts. Work 6 rows straight, ending with a RS row.

Next row: (WS) 1ch, 2dc into first tr, 1dc into each tr to last st, 2dc into 3rd of 3ch, turn. 49[55:61] sts.

Work 3 rows straight. Rep last 4 rows 3 times more. 55[61:67] sts. Work 1 row, ending with a WS row.

Shape armholes:

Next row: (RS) Ss into each of first 4[5:6] sts, 3ch, 1tr into each of next 48[52:56] sts, turn, leaving 3[4:5] sts unworked. 49[53:57] sts.

Next row: 1ch, dc2tog over first 2tr, 1dc into each tr to last 2 sts, dc2tog over next tr and 3rd of 3ch, turn.

Next row: 3ch, miss first st, tr2tog over next 2dc, 1tr into each dc to last 3 sts, tr2tog over next 2dc, 1tr into last st, turn.

Next row: 1ch, 1dc into each st to end, working last dc into 3rd of 3ch, turn.

Rep last 2 rows 2[3:4] times more. 41[43:45] sts.

Work 10 rows straight, ending with a WS row. Fasten off.

Place a marker at each side of centre 19 sts to denote back neck.

LEFT FRONT:

With 5.50mm (UK 5) hook make 28[31:34]ch. Work

foundation row as given for Back (27[30:33] sts), then rep from * to * as given for Back.

Shape side seam:

Next row: (WS) 1ch, 1dc into each tr to last 2 sts, dc2tog over next tr and 3rd of 3ch, turn. 26[29:32] sts.

Work 1 row. Rep last 2 rows 3 times more. 23[26:29] sts. Work 6 rows straight, ending with a RS row.

Next row: (WS) 1ch, 1dc into each tr to last st, 2dc into 3rd of 3ch, turn. 24[27:30] sts.

Work 3 rows straight. Rep last 4 rows 3 times more. 27[30:33] sts. Work 1 row, ending with a WS row.

Shape armhole:

Next row: (RS) Ss into each of first 4[5:6] sts, 3ch, 1tr into each dc to end, turn. 24[26:28] sts.

Next row: 1ch, 1dc into each tr to last 2 sts, dc2tog over next tr and 3rd of 3ch, turn.

Next row: 3ch, miss first st, tr2tog over next 2dc, 1tr into each dc to end, turn.

Next row: 1ch, 1dc into each st to end, working last dc into 3rd of 3ch, turn.

Rep last 2 rows 2[3:4] times more. 20[21:22] sts.

Work 4 rows straight, ending with a WS row.

Shape neck:

Next row: (RS) 3ch, miss first dc, 1tr into each of next 14[15:16]dc, turn leaving 5 sts unworked. 15[16:17] sts.

Next row: 1ch, dc2tog over first 2tr, 1dc into each st to end, working last dc into 3rd of 3ch, turn.

Next row: 3ch, miss first dc, 1tr into each dc to last 2 sts, tr2tog over last 2 sts, turn.

Rep last 2 rows once more. 11[12:13] sts.

Work 1 row. Fasten off.

RIGHT FRONT:

With 5.50mm (UK 5) hook make 43[46:49]ch. Work foundation row as given for Back (42[45:48] sts), then rep from * to * as given for Back.

Shape side seam:

Next row: (WS) 1ch, dc2tog over first 2tr, 1dc into each tr to end, turn. 41[44:47] sts.

Work 1 row. Rep last 2 rows 3 times more. 38[41:44] sts. Work 6 rows straight, ending with a RS row.

Next row: (WS) 1ch, 2dc into first tr, 1dc into each tr,

working last dc into 3rd of 3ch, turn. 39[42:45] sts.
Work 3 rows straight. Rep last 4 rows 1[2:2] times more,
then first 3[1:3] of these 4 rows again, ending with a WS
row. 41[45:48] sts.

Next row: (buttonhole) 3ch, miss first dc, 1tr into next
dc, 1ch, miss 1dc, 1tr into each dc to end, turn.

Next row: 1ch, (2dc into first tr) 1[0:0] times, 1dc into
each st to end, working last dc into 3rd of 3ch, turn.
42[45:48] sts.
Work 4[2:0] rows, ending with a WS row.

Shape armhole:

Work a further 2 buttonholes on every foll 8th row from
previous buttonhole.

Next row: (RS) 3ch, miss first dc, 1tr into each of next
38[40:42]dc, turn leaving 3[4:5] sts unworked. 39[41:43] sts.

Next row: 1ch, dc2tog over first 2tr, 1dc into each tr to
end, working last dc into 3rd of 3ch, turn.

Next row: 3ch, miss first dc, 1tr into each dc to last 3 sts,
tr2tog over next 2dc, 1tr into last st, turn.

Next row: 1ch, 1dc into each st to end, working last dc
into 3rd of 3ch, turn.
Rep last 2 rows 2[3:4] times more. 35[36:37] sts.
Work 4 rows straight, ending with a WS row.
Fasten off.
With RS of work facing, place a marker in 16th st from
beg of next row to mark start of collar.

Shape neck:

Next row: With RS facing, miss first 20 sts, rejoin yarn in
next st, 3ch, 1tr into each dc to end, turn. 15[16:17] sts.

Next row: 1ch, 1dc into each tr to last 2 sts, dc2tog over
next tr and 3rd of 3ch, turn.

Next row: 3ch, miss first st, tr2tog over next 2dc, 1tr into
each dc to end, turn.
Rep last 2 rows once more. 11[12:13] sts.
Work 1 row. Fasten off.

SLEEVES: (make 2)

With 5.50mm (UK 5) hook make 30[32:32]ch. Work
foundation row as given for Back (29[31:31] sts).

Next row: 1ch, 1dc into each dc to end, turn.
Cont in patt as given for Back, work 3 rows, ending with a
RS row.

Shape sides:

Next row: (WS) 1ch, 2dc into first tr, 1dc into each tr to
last st, 2dc into 3rd of 3ch, turn. 31[33:33] sts.
Work 3 rows straight. Rep last 4 rows 1[1:4] times more,
ending with a RS row. 33[35:41] sts. Inc 1 st at each end
of next and every foll 6th row until there are 41[43:45]

sts. Work straight until Sleeve measures 38cm (15in)from
beg, ending with a WS row.

Shape top:

Next row: (RS) Ss into each of first 4[5:6] sts, 3ch,
1tr into each of next 34 sts, turn, leaving 3[4:5] sts
unworked. 35 sts.

Next row: 1ch, dc2tog over first 2tr, 1dc into each tr to
last 2 sts, dc2tog over next tr and 3rd of 3ch, turn.
Work 1 row. Rep last 2 rows 0[2:4] times more, ending
with a RS row. 33[29:25] sts.

Next row: 1ch, dc2tog over first 2tr, 1dc into each tr to
last 2 sts, dc2tog over next tr and 3rd of 3ch, turn.

Next row: 3ch, miss first st, tr2tog over next 2dc, 1tr
into each dc to last 3 sts, tr2tog over next 2dc, 1tr into
last st, turn.
Rep last 2 rows 4[3:2] times more, then work first of
these 2 rows again, ending with a WS row. 11 sts.
Fasten off.

FRONT BORDER:

Join shoulder seams.
With 5.50mm (UK 5) hook and RS facing, rejoin yarn
at lower edge of Right front, 1ch, work in dc evenly up
Right front opening edge, 3dc into corner st, work in dc
around neck, 3dc into corner st (mark centre of these
3dc to mark start of collar), then cont in dc down Left
front opening edge. Fasten off.

COLLAR:

With 5.50mm (UK 5) hook and WS facing, rejoin yarn in
marked st on Left front border, 1ch, 1dc into each dc to
marked st on Right front, turn.

Dec row: 1ch, 1dc into first dc, dc2tog over next 2dc,
1dc into each dc to last 3dc, dc2tog over next 2dc, 1dc
into last dc, turn.

Next row: 1ch, 1dc into each st to end, turn.
Rep dec row once more. Fasten off.

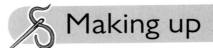

Making up

Press according to directions on ball band. Sew in sleeves,
then join side and sleeve seams. Sew buttons on to left
front to correspond with buttonholes on right front.

Rustic shopping bag

Pack your goodies into this stylish hand-made bag after a trip to the farmers' market.

Basic double crochet worked in cotton yarn on a small hook produces a firm fabric for this stylish two-tone bag that is made in the round without seams.

GETTING STARTED

★★ *Fabric is very easy but working in rounds requires concentration.*

Size:
Bag measures 26cm (10¼in) high x 23cm (9in) in diameter across circular base

How much yarn:
3 x 50g (1¾oz) balls of Rowan Handknit Cotton DK in colour A – Seafarer (shade 318)
4 balls in colour B – Linen (shade 205)

Hook:
3.00mm (UK 11) crochet hook

Tension:
19 sts and 23 rounds measure 10cm (4in) square over dc worked on 3.00mm (UK 11) hook
IT IS ESSENTIAL TO WORK TO THE STATED TENSION TO ACHIEVE SUCCESS

What you have to do:
Starting off with a circle, work in rounds of double crochet throughout. Increase at regular intervals on every round to create circle for bag base. Shape sides of bag with increasing rounds worked at regular intervals. Make buttonhole-style openings for slot handles. Strengthen slots with a second row of stitches worked into gaps.

The Yarn
Rowan Handknit Cotton (approx. 85m/93 yards per 50g/1¾oz ball) is 100% cotton and produces a firm fabric when worked in a basic stitch. The yarn is machine washable and comes in plenty of colours.

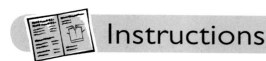

Instructions

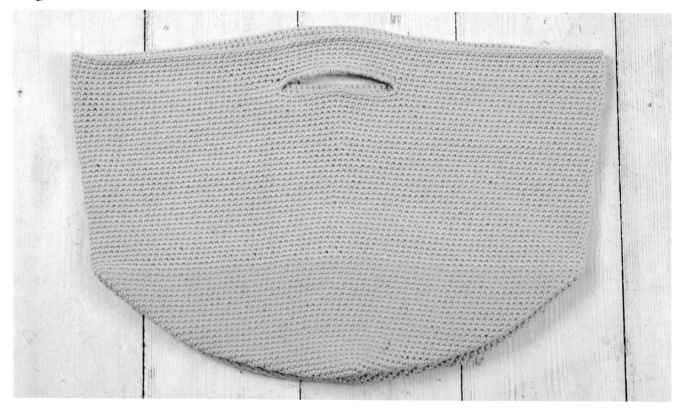

Abbreviations:

ch = chain(s)

cm = centimetre(s)

cont = continue

dc = double crochet

foll = follow(s)(ing)

inc = increasing

rep = repeat

ss = slip stitch

st(s) = stitch(es)

yrh = yarn round hook

BAG:

1st round: With A, make a circle with non-working end of yarn over working end and insert hook into centre, yrh and draw a loop through circle, yrh and draw through a loop, work 6dc in centre of circle, working over 2 ends of yarn, pull on free end of yarn to close circle making sure sts are not twisted, then join with a ss into top of 1st dc. 6 sts. Cont in rounds of dc, inc as foll:

2nd round: 1ch, work 2dc in each st, join with a ss in 1st dc. 12 sts.

3rd round: 1ch, *2dc in next st, 1dc in next st, rep from * to end, join with a ss into 1st dc. 18 sts.

4th round: 1ch, *2dc in next st, 1dc in each of next 2 sts, rep from * to end, join with a ss in 1st dc. 24 sts.

5th round: 1ch, *2dc in next st, 1dc in each of next 3 sts, rep from * to end, join with a ss in 1st dc. 30 sts.

Cont in this way, working 1 more st between increases on every round, until foll

round has been worked:

27th round: 1ch, *2dc in next st, 1dc in each of next 25 sts, rep from * to end, join with a ss in 1st dc. 162 sts.

28th–37th rounds: 1ch, work 1dc in each st to end, join with a ss in 1st dc.

38th round: 1ch, *1dc in each of next 39 sts, 2dc in next st, rep from * to last 3 sts, 1dc in each of next 2 sts, join with a ss in 1st dc. 166 sts.

39th–46th rounds: Work in dc.
Cut off A.

47th round: Join in B and work 1 round in dc.

48th round: 1ch, *1dc in each of next 40 sts, 2dc in next st, rep from * to last 2 sts, 1dc in each of next 2 sts, join with a ss in 1st dc.

49th–57th rounds: Work in dc.

58th round: 1ch, *1dc in each of next 41 sts, 2dc in next st, rep from * to last 2 sts, 1dc in each of last 2 sts, join with a ss in 1st dc. 174 sts.

HOW TO
WORK IN THE ROUND

Instead of working in rows you can work crochet by starting with a central ring and continuing outwards in rounds. The right side of the work will be facing you all the time as you work.

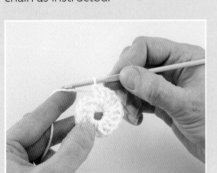

1 Make a yarn loop foundation ring (as described in pattern) or a short chain foundation ring. Hold the bottom of the loop between your thumb and forefinger and make the starting chain as instructed.

2 Work the first round directly into the loop ring.

3 To close the round, work a slip stitch into the top of the starting chain.

4 Make the required starting chain and then continue working the next round making each stitch as instructed by working under both loops of the stitch in the round below.

5 Continue in this way, working each round and joining the rounds with a slip stitch into the starting chain.

6 Working each round as instructed, the number of stitches in each round is increased so that the circle of stitches grows in size.

59th–67th rounds: Work in dc.

68th round: 1ch, *1dc in each of next 42 sts, 2dc in next st, rep from * to last 2 sts, 1dc in each of last 2 sts, join with a ss in 1st dc. 178 sts.

69th–77th rounds: Work in dc.

78th round: 1ch, *1dc in each of next 43 sts, 2dc in next st, rep from * to last 2 sts, 1dc in each of last 2 sts, join with a ss in 1st dc. 182 sts.

Make slot handle:

Next round: 1ch, 1dc in each of next 35 sts, 20ch, miss 20 sts, 1dc in each of next 71 sts, 20ch, miss 20 sts, 1dc in

each of next 36 sts, join with a ss in 1st dc.

Next round: Work in dc, working 20dc into each 20ch space.

Next round: Work in dc, working 20 sts into each handle slot again (rather than into tops of sts) and working dc 1 row down at ends of handle slots.

Work 7 more rounds in dc. Fasten off.

Light-as-a-feather wrap

A simple horizontal stitch pattern worked in a mohair yarn creates a romantic wrap.

Worked in alternating blocks of raised trebles and a beautiful brushed yarn, this wrap lightly gathers up in ridges along its length when worn.

GETTING STARTED

⭐ *Working raised trebles may take some practice, but the rest is straightforward.*

Size:
Wrap measures approximately 39 x 120cm
(5½ x 47in)

How much yarn:
4 x 25g (1oz) balls of GGH Kid-Melange in Raspberry Pink (shade 023)

Hook:
4.00mm (UK 8) crochet hook

Tension:
20 sts and 14 rows measure 10cm (4in) square over patt on 4.00mm (UK 8) hook
IT IS ESSENTIAL TO WORK TO THE STATED TENSION TO ACHIEVE SUCCESS

What you have to do:
Work foundation row of trebles. Continue in two-row pattern of raised trebles, alternating to front and back to create a ridged effect.

The Yarn
GGH Kid Melange (approx. 250m/273 yards per 25g/1oz ball) is 65% kid mohair, 30% polyamide and 5% wool. Handwash only, it is a fine mohair yarn with a rich depth of colour in a range of shades.

Instructions

Abbreviations:

ch = chain
cm = centimetre(s)
patt = pattern
rep = repeat
RS = right side
st(s) = stitch(es)
tr = treble
yrh = yarn round hook

WRAP:

With 4.00mm (UK 8) hook make 80ch.

Foundation row: 1tr into 4th ch from hook, 1tr into each ch to end, turn. 78 sts.

1st row: (RS) 3ch (counts as first tr), miss tr at base of ch, yrh, insert hook from front and from right to left around post of next tr, yrh and complete tr in usual way – called raised tr front (rtrf), 1rtrf around each of next 4 sts, *yrh, insert hook from back and from right to left around post of next tr, yrh and complete tr in usual way – called raised tr back (rtrb), 1rtrb around each of next 5 sts, 1rtrf around each of next 6 sts, rep from * to end, working last rtrf around 3ch, turn.

2nd row: 3ch, miss tr at base of ch, 1rtrb around each of next 5 sts, *1rtrf around each of next 6 sts, 1rtrb around each of next 6 sts, rep from * to end, working last rtrb around 3ch, turn.

The last 2 rows form patt. Rep them until work measures approximately 120cm (47in), or length required. Fasten off.

HOW TO
WORK RELIEF TREBLES

Relief stitches are worked around the post of a stitch instead of into the loops on the top of the stitch and they make a very textured pattern. In this wrap, bands of relief trebles are worked across the rows to give the horizontal stripes.

3 To work a relief treble back (rtrb), wrap the yarn around the hook and insert the hook from the back and from the right to left around the post of the next stitch. Tip the work towards you as you do this so you can see the back of the fabric.

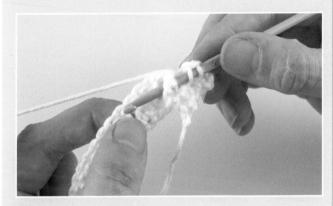

1 To work a relief treble front (rtrf), wrap the yarn around the hook and insert the hook from the front and from the right to left around the post of the next stitch.

4 To complete the stitch work the rest of the treble in the usual way by wrapping the yarn around the hook, drawing through a loop, wrapping the yarn around the hook and drawing through the first two loops and then wrapping the yarn around the hook again and drawing through the remaining two loops on the hook.

2 To complete the stitch work the rest of the treble in the usual way by wrapping the yarn around the hook, drawing through a loop, wrapping the yarn around the hook and drawing through the first two loops and then wrapping the yarn around the hook again and drawing through the remaining two loops on the hook.

Multi-colour cushion

The wonderfully named 'wiggly crochet' is the highly effective technique used here!

Trebles in colourful shades worked on top of a mesh grid form a wiggly shape and a rich, dense pattern on this cushion. The back is a plain granny square.

GETTING STARTED

★★★ *Basic cushion is easy to work but wiggly crochet requires patience and practice.*

Size:
40cm (16in) square

How much yarn:
2 x 100g (3½oz) hanks of Artesano Aran in colour A – Strathy (shade SFN10)
1 hank in each of seven other colours: B – Lomond (shade 5083); C – Calder (shade 5167); D – Fleet (shade 5570); E – Inchard (shade 6315); F – Ochre (shade C810); G – Wester (shade 0042) and H – Royal blue (shade C963)

Hooks:
4.50mm (UK 7) crochet hook
5.00mm (UK 6) crochet hook

Additional item:
40cm (16in) square cushion pad

Tension:
16 sts (8 squares) and 8 rows measure 10cm (4in) square over mesh patt on 4.50mm (UK 7) hook
IT IS ESSENTIAL TO WORK TO THE STATED TENSION TO ACHIEVE SUCCESS

What you have to do:
Work cushion front in basic filet mesh in main colour only. Work cushion back as a large granny square in main colour. Use eight colours to cover entire cushion front with wiggly crochet, working trebles that stand up in relief.

The Yarn
Artesano Aran (approx. 132m/ 144 yards per 100g/ 3½oz ball) is a blend of 50% each of alpaca and Peruvian highland wool. It produces a soft, warm fabric, and comes in many colours.

 Instructions

CUSHION FRONT:
With 4.50mm (UK 7) hook and A, make 50ch.
Foundation row: (RS) 1tr into 6th ch from hook, *1ch, miss 1ch, 1tr into next ch, rep from * to end, turn. 23 squares.
Patt row: 4ch (counts as first tr and 1ch sp), miss first sp, 1tr into next tr, *1ch, 1tr into next tr, rep from * to

Abbreviations:
ch = chain(s)
cm = centimetre(s)
cont = continue
patt = pattern
rep = repeat
RS = right side
sp(s) = space(s)
ss = slip stitch
st(s) = stitch(es)
tr = treble
WS = wrong side

end working last tr into 4th of 5ch (and 3rd of 4ch on subsequent rows), turn. Rep last row 21 times more. 23 rows in total. Fasten off.

CUSHION BACK:
With 5.00mm (UK 6) hook and A, make 4ch, join with a ss into first ch to form a ring.

1st round: 3ch (counts as first tr), 2tr into ring, 2ch, (3tr into ring, 2ch) 3 times, join with a ss into 3rd of 3ch.

2nd round: 3ch, miss st at base of ch, 1tr into each of next 2tr, (2tr, 2ch, 2tr) into 2ch (corner) sp, (1tr into each of next 3tr, (2tr, 2ch, 2tr) into next 2ch sp) 3 times, join with a ss into 3rd of 3ch.

3rd round: 3ch, miss st at base of ch, 1tr into each of next 4tr, (2tr, 2ch, 2tr) into 2ch sp, (1tr into each of next 7tr, (2tr, 2ch, 2tr) into next 2ch sp) 3 times, 1tr into each of next 2tr, join with a ss into 3rd of 3ch.

4th round: 3ch, miss st at base of ch, 1tr into each of next 6tr, (2tr, 2ch, 2tr) into 2ch sp, (1tr into each of next 11tr, (2tr, 2ch, 2tr) in next 2ch sp) 3 times, 1tr into each of next 4tr, join with a ss into 3rd of 3ch.

5th round: 3ch, miss st at base of ch, 1tr into each of next 8tr, (2tr, 2ch, 2tr) into 2ch sp, (1tr into each of next 15tr, (2tr, 2ch, 2tr) in next 2ch sp) 3 times, 1tr into each of next 6tr, join with a ss into 3rd of 3ch.

6th round: 3ch, miss st at base of ch, 1tr into each of next 10tr, (2tr, 2ch, 2tr) into 2ch sp, (1tr into each of next 19tr, (2tr, 2ch, 2tr) in next 2ch sp) 3 times, 1tr into each of next 8tr, join with a ss into 3rd of 3ch.

7th round: 3ch, miss st at base of ch, 1tr into each of next 12tr, (2tr, 2ch, 2tr) into 2ch sp, (1tr into each of next 23tr, (2tr, 2ch, 2tr) in next 2ch sp) 3 times, 1tr into each of next 10tr, join with a ss into 3rd of 3ch.

8th round: 3ch, miss st at base of ch, 1tr into each of next 14tr, (2tr, 2ch, 2tr) into

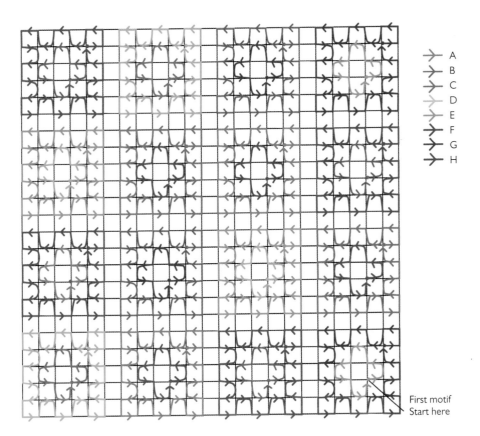

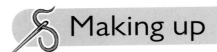

First motif
Start here

2ch sp, (1tr into each of next 27tr, (2tr, 2ch, 2tr) in next 2ch sp) 3 times, 1tr into each of next 12tr, join with a ss into 3rd of 3ch.

9th round: 3ch, miss st at base of ch, 1tr into each of next 16tr, (2tr, 2ch, 2tr) into 2ch sp, (1tr into each of next 31tr, (2tr, 2ch, 2tr) in next 2ch sp) 3 times, 1tr into each of next 14tr, join with a ss into 3rd of 3ch.

10th round: 3ch, miss st at base of ch, 1tr into each of next 18tr, (2tr, 2ch, 2tr) into 2ch sp, (1tr into each of next 35tr, (2tr, 2ch, 2tr) in next 2ch sp) 3 times, 1tr into each of next 16tr, join with a ss into 3rd of 3ch. Fasten off.

WIGGLY CROCHET:

Note: Each motif comprises an inner cross in one colour and an outer cross in a contrasting colour. Always work inner cross first. Tr sts of wiggly crochet are perpendicular to mesh background.

First motif:

With RS of mesh Cushion Front facing, 4.50mm (UK 7) hook and using diagram as reference, join E to base of 2nd square in 3rd row at lower right-hand corner, 3ch (counts as first tr), 4tr over 1ch at base of square, turn work through 90 degrees and work 5tr over stem of tr at side of square, turn work through 90 degrees and work 5tr over 1ch at top of square, cont in this way,

working around outline of inner cross, join with a ss into 3rd of 3ch. Fasten off.

Join G to base of 2nd square in 2nd row at lower right-hand corner as indicated on diagram and outline outer cross in same way. Using diagram as a guide, cont until all motifs have been worked on Cushion Front.

Making up

With WS facing, place Cushion front on to Cushion back. With A, whip stitch together around 3 sides, working carefully between tr sts of wiggly crochet, but do not fasten off. Insert cushion pad and sew last side closed.

Chevron scarf

This oversize scarf looks great especially when worked in warm, autumnal colours.

This classic long scarf with fringes is worked in a sharp chevron pattern throughout and highlighted at each end with toning stripes in graduated widths.

GETTING STARTED

 There is only one pattern row throughout, which soon becomes familiar.

Size:
Scarf measures 24cm (9½in) wide x 153cm (60in) long, excluding fringing

How much yarn:
5 x 50g (1¾oz) balls of Debbie Bliss Fez in colour A – Rust (shade 08)
2 balls in colour B – Peach (shade 09)

Hook:
5.00mm (UK 6) crochet hook

Tension:
14 sts (1 patt rep) measures 8cm (3⅛in) and 7 rows measure 10cm (4in) on 5.00mm (UK 6) hook
IT IS ESSENTIAL TO WORK TO THE STATED TENSION TO ACHIEVE SUCCESS

What you have to do:
Make a length of foundation chain very loosely. Work throughout in trebles, creating chevron pattern by mass increasing and decreasing stitches at regular intervals throughout each row. Work a two-colour stripe sequence at each end of scarf. Knot tassels into points and indentations of chevron pattern.

The Yarn
Debbie Bliss Fez (approx. 100m/109 yards per 50g/1¾oz ball) contains 85% extra fine merino wool and 15% camel in an aran-weight yarn. The fabric, washable at low temperature, feels luxurious. There are plenty of colours available.

Instructions

Abbreviations:

beg = beginning

ch = chain(s)

cm = centimetre(s)

patt = pattern

rep = repeat

RS = right side

st(s) = stitch(es)

tr = treble(s)

tr3tog = work 1tr in each of next 3 sts leaving last loop of each on hook, yarn round hook and draw through all 4 loops

SCARF:

With 5.00mm (UK 6) hook and A, make 45ch very loosely.

Foundation row: (RS) 2tr into 4th ch from hook, *1tr into each of next 3ch, (over next 3ch work tr3tog) twice, 1tr into each of next 3ch, 3tr into each of next 2ch, rep from * ending last rep with 3tr once into last ch, turn. 42 sts.

Patt row: 3ch (counts as first tr), 2tr into st at base of ch, *1tr into each of next 3tr, (over next 3 sts work tr3tog) twice, 1tr into each of next 3tr, 3tr into each of next 2tr, rep from * ending last rep with 3tr once into top of 3ch, turn.

Rep patt row twice more, joining in B for final part of last st in last row.

Rep patt row throughout to form patt, working in stripe sequence of 4 rows B, 3 rows A, 3 rows B, 2 rows A, 2 rows B, 1 row A and 1 row B. Now cont in A only until

work measures approximately 124cm (49in) from beg, ending with a RS row.
Work stripe sequence of 1 row B, 1 row A, 2 rows B, 2 rows A, 3 rows B, 3 rows A, 4 rows B and 4 rows A. Fasten off.

Tassels:

Cut 5 x 45cm (18in) lengths of A for each tassel. Knot a tassel in each point and indentation of chevrons across short ends of Scarf. Trim tassels evenly. Press Scarf lightly according to directions on ball band.

HOW TO
CHANGE COLOUR

For the striped panels, start the new colour on the last stitch in the old colour as shown in detail below.

1 Work to the last treble stitch in the row before you need to change colour. Work the stitch as follows. Wrap the yarn around hook and insert in the last stitch. Catch the yarn and draw the loop through the stitch (three loops on the hook) take the yarn around the hook and draw through two of the loops.

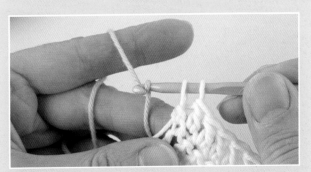

2 Drop the working yarn and wrap the new yarn around the hook. Draw through the two loops on the hook, which are in the old yarn, to complete the stitch.

3 Work the three chain stitches that form the turning chain with the new colour and then proceed to work the next row in the new colour as instructed. Each colour change is made in this way.

Soft fitted jacket

Styled to look like a tailored jacket, this design is soft
and snug and crocheted in alpaca fibres.

With its nipped-in waist, three-quarter length sleeves and collar with lapels, this stylish fitted jacket has a neat patterned fabric that is easy to work.

The Yarn

King Cole Baby Alpaca (approx. 100m/109 yards per 50g/1¾oz ball) is a double knitting weight that contains 100% alpaca fibres. It is very soft and has a small range of mainly natural shades.

GETTING STARTED

★ ★ ★ *Although pattern is easy to follow once established, there is a lot of challenging shaping.*

Size:
To fit bust: 81–86[91–97:102–107]cm (32–34[36–38:40–42]in)
Actual size: 94[103:114]cm (37[40½:45]in)
Length: 55[58:59]cm (29½[22¾:23¼]in)
Sleeve seam: 31[32:33]cm (12¼[12½:13]in)
Note: Figures in square brackets [ ] refer to larger sizes; where there is only one set of figures, it applies to all sizes

How much yarn:
16[17:18] x 50g (1¾oz) balls of King Cole Baby Alpaca in Camel (shade 500)

Hook:
4.00mm (UK 8) crochet hook

Additional items:
3 buttons, Stitch markers

Tension:
19.5 sts measure 10cm (4in) and 12 rows measure 9cm (3½in) over patt on 4.00mm (UK 8) hook
IT IS ESSENTIAL TO WORK TO THE STATED TENSION TO ACHIEVE SUCCESS

What you have to do:
Work throughout in cluster pattern with double crochet for collar, revers and edgings. Shape side edges for fitted style. Shape lower edges of fronts for cut-away style. Use turning rows to shape lapel.

 # Instructions

Abbreviations:

alt = alternate; **beg** = beginning; **ch** = chain(s)
cm = centimetre(s); **cont** = continue
dc = double crochet; **dec** = decrease(ing) as foll: (yrh, insert hook into next st, yrh and draw a loop through, yrh and draw through first two loops on hook) twice, yrh and draw through all 3 loops **foll** = follow(s)(ing);
htr = half treble; **inc** = increase(ing) as foll: work 2 sts into one st or ch sp; **patt** = pattern; **rep** = repeat
RS = right side; **sp** = space; **ss** = slip stitch
st(s) = stitch(es); **tog** = together; **tr** = treble(s)
WS = wrong side; **yrh** = yarn round hook

BACK:
With 4.00mm (UK 8) hook make 94[104:114]ch.
Foundation row: (WS) 1dc into 2nd ch from hook, *1ch, miss 1ch, 1dc into next ch, rep from * to end, turn. 93[103:113] sts.
1st row: (RS) 3ch (counts as first tr), *into next ch sp work (yrh, insert into ch sp, yrh and draw a loop through, yrh and

draw through first two loops on hook) 3 times – called tr3tog, 1ch, miss 1dc, rep from * ending with tr3tog into last ch sp, 1tr into last dc, turn.

2nd row: 1ch (does not count as a st), 1dc into st at base of ch, *1ch, miss 1 st, 1dc into next ch sp, rep from * ending with 1dc into 3rd of 3ch, turn. Rep last 2 rows to form patt. Cont in patt, dec 1 st at each end of 3rd row and 3 foll 4th rows. 85[95:105] sts. Work 7 rows straight. Now inc 1 st at each end of next and 3 foll 4th rows. 93[103:113] sts. Work 9 rows straight, ending with a WS row.

Shape armholes:

Next row: Ss into each of first 9 sts, patt to last 8 sts, turn. 77[87:97] sts.

Work a further 23[27:29] rows straight. Fasten off. Mark centre 29[31:33] sts for back neck.

RIGHT FRONT:

With 4.00mm (UK 8) hook make 24[28:34]ch.

Foundation row: (WS) 1dc into 2nd ch from hook, *1ch, miss 1ch, 1dc into next ch, rep from * to end, turn. 23[27:33] sts.

1st row: (RS) 6ch, 1dc into 2nd ch from hook, 1ch, miss 1ch, into next ch work (yrh, insert hook into next st and draw through a loop) 3 times, yrh and draw through all 7 loops on hook – called htr3tog, 1ch, miss next ch, tr3tog into next ch, *1ch, miss next st, tr3tog into next ch sp, rep from * to last st, 1tr into last dc, turn.

2nd row: 1ch (does not count as a st), 1dc into st at base of ch, *1ch, miss 1 st, 1dc into next ch sp, rep from * ending 1ch, 1dc into turning ch, turn.

3rd row: As 1st row.

4th row: As 2nd row. 35[39:45] sts.

5th row: 3ch (counts as first tr), 1ch (inc made), patt to last 3 sts, tr2tog into next 2 sts (dec made), 1tr into last dc, turn. 35[39:45] sts.

6th row: 1ch, 1dc into st at base of ch, 1dc into dec on previous row, *1ch, miss next st, 1dc into next ch sp, rep

from * to last st, 1ch (inc made), 1dc into 3rd of 3ch, turn. 36[40:46] sts. **Cont in this way, inc 1 st at front edge on next 2 rows, then on 4 foll alt rows, AT SAME TIME dec 1 st at side edge of 3rd row and 2 foll 4th rows. 39[43:49] sts. Work 7 rows straight.

Keeping front edge straight, inc 1 st at side edge on next and 3 foll 4th rows. 43[47:53] sts. Work 6 rows straight, ending with a RS row. Place a marker at beg of last row.

Shape front slope:

Next row: Dec 1 st at front slope on next and foll alt row, ending with a WS row. 41[45:51] sts.

Shape armhole:

Next row: Patt to last 8 sts, turn. 33[37:43] sts.

Keeping armhole edge straight, cont to dec 1 st at front slope on next and 8[9:10] foll alt rows. 24[27:32] sts. Work 4[6:6] rows straight. Fasten off.

LEFT FRONT:

With 4.00mm (UK 8) hook make 29[33:39]ch.

Foundation row: (WS) Ss into each of first 6ch, *1dc into next ch, 1ch, miss next ch, rep from * to last ch, 1dc into last ch, turn. 23[27:33] sts.

1st row: (RS) 3ch (counts as first tr), *tr3tog into next ch sp, 1ch, miss next dc, rep from * to last 6 sts, (tr3tog into next st, 1ch, miss next st) twice, htr3tog into next st, 1dc into last st, turn.

2nd row: 6ch, ss into each of first 6ch, 1dc into next st, *1ch, miss next st, 1dc into next ch sp, rep from * to last 2 sts, 1ch, miss next st, 1dc into 3rd of 3ch, turn.

3rd row: As 1st row. 35[39:45] sts.

4th row: 1ch, 1dc into st at base of ch, *1ch, miss next st, 1dc into next ch sp, rep from * to last 2 sts, 1ch, miss next st, 1dc into 3rd of 3ch, turn.

5th row: 3ch, tr2tog over next ch sp and dc (dec made), *tr3tog into next ch sp, 1ch, miss next dc, rep from * to last 2 sts, tr3tog into last ch sp, 1ch (inc made), 1tr into last dc, turn. 35[39:45] sts.

6th row: 1ch, 1dc into st at base of ch, 1ch (inc made), 1dc into ch sp, 1ch, miss next st, *1dc into next ch sp, 1ch, miss next st, rep from * ending with 1dc into last st, turn. 36[40:46] sts.

Complete as given for Right front from ** to end.

SLEEVES: (make 2)

With 4.00mm (UK 8) hook make 52[56:60]ch.

Foundation row: (WS) 1dc into 2nd ch from hook, *1ch, miss 1ch, 1dc into next ch, rep from * to end, turn. 51[55:59] sts.

Cont in patt as given for Back, AT SAME TIME inc 1 st at each end of foll 6[7:8] alt rows (63[69:75] sts), then on 6 foll 4th rows. 75[81:87] sts. Work straight until Sleeve measures 30[31:32]cm (11¾[12:12½]in) from beg. Place a marker at each end of last row. Work 6 more rows straight. Fasten off.

BUTTON BAND AND LAPEL:

With 4.00mm (UK 8) hook and RS of work facing, rejoin yarn to Left Front at top of 14th[16th:18th] row up from marker for beg of front slope shaping.

Next row: 1 ch (does not count as a st), work 8dc into row ends of next 4 rows, turn.

Next row: 1 ch, 1 dc into each of previous 8dc, turn.

Next row: 1 ch, 1 dc into each of previous 8dc, then work 8dc into row ends of next 4 rows, turn.

Next row: 1 ch, 1 dc into each of previous 16dc, turn.
Cont in this way, working 8 more dc on each RS row and working back over these sts on WS row until 24[32:32] sts have been worked, ending with a WS row.

1st and 3rd sizes only:

Next row: 1 ch, 1 dc into each of next 24[32] sts, then work 3dc into row ends of next 2 rows, turn.

Next row: 1 ch, 1 dc into each of previous 27[35] sts, turn.

All sizes:

Next row: 1 ch, 1 dc into each of next 27[32:35] sts, work in dc evenly along Left front to side edge, turn.
Work 4 more rows in dc. Fasten off.

Mark positions on button band for 3 buttons, the first in line with last inc row on front curve and the last 2cm (¾in) down from beg of front slope shaping, with the other evenly spaced between.

BUTTONHOLE BAND AND LAPEL:

With 4.00mm (UK 8) hook and RS of work facing, rejoin yarn to Right Front at top of 10th[12th:14th] row up from marker for beg of front slope shaping and work 8dc evenly along row ends of next 4 rows, turn.

Next row: 1 ch, 1 dc into each of previous 8dc, then work 8dc into row ends of next 4 rows, turn.

Next row: 1 ch, 1 dc into each of previous 16dc, turn.

Next row: 1 ch, 1 dc into each of previous 16dc, then work 8dc into row ends of next 4 rows, turn.

Next row: 1 ch, 1 dc into each of previous 24dc, turn.

2nd and 3rd sizes only:

Next row: 1 ch, 1 dc into each of previous 24dc, then work 8dc into row ends of next 4 rows, turn.

3rd size only:

Next row: 1 ch, 1 dc into each of previous 32dc, turn.

1st and 3rd sizes only:

Next row: 1 ch, 1 dc into each of previous 24[32]dc, then work 3dc into row ends of next 2 rows.

All sizes:

27[32:35]dc. Fasten off.
With 4.00mm (UK 8) hook and RS of work facing, rejoin yarn at side edge, 1 ch, work in dc evenly along Right front edge, then work in dc across 27[32:35] sts on rever, turn.

Buttonhole row: Work in dc, making buttonholes to correspond with markers by working 2ch, miss 2dc.

Next row: Work in dc, working 2dc into each 2ch sp on previous row, turn.
Work 2 more rows in dc. Fasten off.

COLLAR:

Join shoulder seams.
With 4.00mm (UK 8) hook and WS of work facing, work 29[31:33]dc across back neck, turn.

** Next row: 1 ch, 1 dc into each dc to end, then work 4dc down row ends on next 2 patt rows on Left front, turn.

Next row: 1 ch, 1 dc into each dc to end, then work 4dc down row ends on next 2 patt rows on Right front, turn.**
Rep from ** to ** 4[5:5] times more. Work 2 more rows in same way but working 5 sts from last 3 rows on each Front. 87[99:103] sts.
Work 8[10:12] rows in dc, inc 1 st at each end of every foll alt row and ss to corresponding row on top edge of lapels as you work. 89[93:97] sts. Work 6 rows straight, without ss to lapels. Fasten off.

BACK HEM EDGE:

With 4.00mm (UK 8) hook and RS of work facing, rejoin yarn to lower edge of Back, 1 ch, work evenly in dc along lower edge, turn. Work 4 more rows in dc. Fasten off.

CUFF EDGE:

With 4.00mm (UK 8) hook and RS of work facing, rejoin yarn to lower edge of Sleeve, 1 ch, work evenly in dc along cuff edge, turn. Work 1 more row in dc. Fasten off.

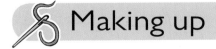

Making up

Sew in sleeves, joining rows ends above markers to sts at underarms. Join side and sleeve seams. Sew on buttons.

Giant granny-square throw

You'll be a granny-square expert once you have completed this colourful throw.

Worked in a chunky yarn and subtly striped in colours that blend and some strong accent shades, the original granny-square motif at the centre of this will soon grow into a giant throw.

The Yarn

King Cole Merino Blend Chunky (approx. 67m/73 yards per 50g/1¾oz ball) contains 100% pure new wool. It produces a soft, machine-washable fabric. The shade range includes both strong and subtle colours.

GETTING STARTED

Pattern is easy to follow once you get started but you will need patience to achieve such a large size.

Size:

Approximately 127cm (50in) x 127cm (50in)

How much yarn:

3 x 50g (1¾oz) balls of King Cole Merino Blend Chunky in each of two colours: A – Raspberry (shade 915) and B – Plum (shade 916)

4 balls in each of two colours: C – Cream (shade 919) and D – Silver (shade 918)

5 balls in colour E – Eucalyptus (shade 914)

6 balls in colour F – Pebble (shade 909)

Hook:

5.50mm (UK 5) crochet hook

Tension:

13 sts and 7.5 rows measure 10cm (4in) square over tr on 5.50mm (UK 5) hook

IT IS ESSENTIAL TO WORK TO THE STATED TENSION TO ACHIEVE SUCCESS

What you have to do:

Start at centre of square and work in rounds of trebles with a chain space at centre of each side of square and another at each corner. Work in stripes of colours as directed. Work outer edging in double crochet.

Instructions

Abbreviations:

ch = chain(s)
cm = centimetre(s)
cont = continue
dc = double crochet
foll = follows
patt = pattern
rep = repeat
sp = space
ss = slip stitch
tr = treble

THROW:

With 5.50mm (UK 5) hook and A, make 4ch, join with a ss into first ch to form a ring.

1st round: 3ch (counts as 1tr), 3tr into ring, 3ch, (4tr into ring, 3ch) 3 times, join with a ss into 3rd of 3ch.

2nd round: 5ch (counts as 1tr, 2ch), miss st at base of ch, *(miss next 2tr, 1tr into next tr, (2tr, 3ch, 2tr) into 3ch sp at corner **, 1tr into next tr, 2ch, rep from * 3 times more, ending last rep at **, join with a ss into 3rd of 5ch. Fasten off A.

3rd round: Join C to same place as last ss, 5ch, miss next 2ch sp, 1tr into each of next 3tr, (2tr, 3ch, 2tr) into 3ch sp at corner, *1tr into each of next 3tr, 2ch, 1tr

into each of next 3tr, (2tr, 3ch, 2tr) into 3ch sp at corner, rep from * twice more, 1tr into each of next 2tr, join with a ss into 3rd of 5ch.

4th round: With C, 5ch, miss next 2ch sp, 1tr into each of next 5tr, (2tr, 3ch, 2tr) into 3ch sp at corner, *1tr into each of next 5tr, 2ch, 1tr into each of next 5tr, (2tr, 3ch, 2tr) into 3ch sp at corner, rep from * twice more, 1tr into each of next 4tr, join with a ss into 3rd of 5ch. Fasten off C.

5th round: Join D to same place as last ss, 5ch, miss next 2ch sp, 1tr into each of next 7tr, (2tr, 3ch, 2tr) into 3ch sp at corner, *1tr into each of next 7tr, 2ch, 1tr into each of next 7tr, (2tr, 3ch, 2tr) into 3ch sp at corner, rep from * twice more,

1tr into each of next 6tr, join with a ss into 3rd of 5ch.
6th round: With D, 5ch, miss next 2ch sp, 1tr into each of next 9tr, (2tr, 3ch, 2tr) into 3ch sp at corner, *1tr into each of next 9tr, 2ch, 1tr into each of next 9tr, (2tr, 3ch, 2tr) into 3ch sp at corner, rep from * twice more, 1tr into each of next 8tr, join with a ss into 3rd of 5ch. Fasten off D.

Cont in patt as now set, increasing by working an extra 2tr at each side of centre 2ch sp and (2tr, 3ch, 2tr) into each corner sp and working stripes as foll:

2 rounds E, 2 round F, 1 round A, 1 round B, *3 rounds C, 3 rounds D, 3 rounds E, 3 rounds F, 1 round A *, 1 round B, then rep from * to * once more. Fasten off.

Edging:

Next round: Join B to next 2ch sp, 1ch (does not count as a st), 2dc into 2ch sp, 1dc into each tr all round, working 2dc into each 2ch sp at centre and (2dc, 3ch, 2dc) into each corner sp, join with a ss into first dc.

Next round: 1ch, 1dc into each dc all round, working (2dc, 3ch, 2dc) into each corner sp, join with a ss into first dc. Fasten off.

Circular pattern beret

Pull on this cosy beret for a winter walk.

Get back to nature with this 'big' beret with a ribbed brim worked in a pure wool eco yarn and a circular pattern of raised trebles.

GETTING STARTED

★★ *The slightly unusual construction of this beret requires concentration.*

Size:
To fit an average-sized adult head

How much yarn:
3 x 50g (1¾oz) balls of Sirdar Eco Wool DK in Flint (shade 204)

Hooks:
3.50mm (UK 9) crochet hook
4.50mm (UK 7) crochet hook

Tension:
16 sts and 11 rounds measure 10cm (4in) square over patt on 4.50mm (UK 7) hook
IT IS ESSENTIAL TO WORK TO THE STATED TENSION TO ACHIEVE SUCCESS

What you have to do:
Work brim first in rows of ridged double crochet rib pattern. Work into row-ends of brim to start working main part in rounds of alternating trebles and raised treble pattern. Shape main part by deceasing towards centre of crown as directed.

The Yarn
Sirdar Eco Wool DK (approx. 100m/109 yards per 50g/1¾oz ball) is 100% pure wool. Available in a small selection of natural shades (some variegated), this yarn produces a soft hand-wash-only fabric.

Instructions

Abbreviations:

ch = chain(s)
cm = centimetre(s)
cont = continue
dc = double crochet
dec = decrease
foll = follows
inc = increase
patt = pattern
rep = repeat
rtrb = work raised treble at back as foll: yrh, insert hook from back and from right to left around stem of appropriate st, yrh and draw a loop through, (yrh and draw through 2 loops on hook) twice
ss = slip stitch
st(s) = stitch(es)
tr = treble
tr2tog = work 1 tr into each of next 2 sts leaving last loop of each on hook, yrh and draw through all 3 loops on hook
WS = wrong side
yrh = yarn round hook

BERET
Brim:

With 3.50mm (UK 9) hook make 8ch.
Foundation row: 1dc into 2nd ch from hook, 1dc into each ch to end, turn. 8 sts.
Rib patt row: 1ch (counts as first dc), miss st at base of ch, 1dc into back loop only of each st to end, working last dc into turning ch, turn.
Work a further 86 rows in rib patt; do not turn at end of last row.

Main part:

Change to 4.50mm (UK 7) hook.
Turn work on side and cont as foll: 1ch (counts as first dc), miss first row end, 1dc into each row end, join with a ss into first ch, turn. 88 sts.
Inc round: (WS) 3ch (counts as first tr), miss st at base of ch, *(2tr into next st, 1tr

into each of next 3 sts) twice, 2tr into next st, 1tr into each of next 2 sts, rep from * 6 times more, (2tr into next st, 1tr into each of next 3 sts) twice, 2tr into next st, 1tr into last st, join with a ss into 3rd of 3ch, turn. 112 sts.

1st round: 3ch, miss st at base of ch, 1rtrb into each st to end, join with a ss into 3rd of 3ch, turn.

2nd round: 3ch, miss st at base of ch, 1tr into each st to end, join with a ss into 3rd of 3ch, turn.

The last 2 rounds form patt. Rep them twice more and then work 1st round again.

1st dec round: 3ch, miss st at base of ch, 1tr into each of next 2 sts, *tr2tog over next 2 sts, 1tr into each of next 5 sts, rep from * 14 times more, tr2tog over next 2 sts, 1tr into each of next 2 sts, join with a ss into 3rd of 3ch, turn. 96 sts.

Patt 1 round.

2nd dec round: 3ch, miss st at base of ch, 1tr into next st, *tr2tog over next 2 sts, 1tr into each of next 4 sts, rep from * 14 times more, tr2tog over next 2 sts, 1tr into each of next 2 sts, join with a ss into 3rd of 3ch, turn. 80 sts.

Patt 1 round.

3rd dec round: 3ch, miss st at base of ch, 1tr into next st, *tr2tog over next 2 sts, 1tr into each of next 3 sts, rep from * 14 times more, tr2tog over next 2 sts, 1tr into next st, join with a ss into 3rd of 3ch, turn. 64 sts.

Patt 1 round.

4th dec round: 3ch, miss st at base of ch, *tr2tog over next 2 sts, 1tr into each of next 2 sts, rep from * 14 times more, tr2tog over next 2 sts, 1tr into next st, join with a ss into 3rd of 3ch, turn. 48 sts.

Patt 1 round.

5th dec round: 3ch, miss st at base of ch, *tr2tog over next 2 sts, rep from * 22 times more, 1tr into last st, join with a ss into 3rd of 3ch, turn. 25 sts.

Patt 1 round.

6th dec round: 3ch, miss st at base of ch, *tr2tog over next 2 sts, rep from * 11 times more, join with a ss into 3rd of 3ch. 13 sts. Fasten off, leaving a long end of yarn.

 # Making up

Weave long end of yarn through top of remaining 13 sts, pull up tightly and fasten off securely. Join first and last rows on brim.

Man's funnel-neck sweater

Crochet this stylish sweater to make a weekend favourite for the man in your life.

This fabulous sweater is worked in a mock-rib pattern throughout to produce a spectacular chunky fabric, and has up-to-the-minute styling, which includes an unusual opening with a buttoned collar.

The Yarn

Debbie Bliss Cashmerino Aran (approx. 90m/ 98 yards per 50g/1¾oz ball) is 55% merino wool, 33% microfibre and 12% cashmere. This produces a soft and luxurious fabric that can be hand-washed at a low temperature. There is a wide range of fabulous colours to suit everyone.

GETTING STARTED

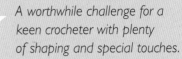

A worthwhile challenge for a keen crocheter with plenty of shaping and special touches.

Size:
To fit chest: 91[96:102:106]cm (36[38:40:42]in)
Actual size: 102[107:112:117]cm (40[42:44:46]in)
Length: 61[63:64.5:66.5]cm (24[24¾:25½;26½]in)
Sleeve seam: 46[47.5:49:50.5]cm
(18[18¾:19¼:20]in)
Note: Figures in square brackets [ ] refer to larger sizes; where there is only one set of figures, it applies to all sizes
How much yarn:
22[23:25:26] x 50g (1¾oz) balls of Debbie Bliss Cashmerino Aran in Teal Blue (shade 205)
Hooks:
4.00mm (UK 8) crochet hook
5.00mm (UK 6) crochet hook
Additional item:
3 medium buttons
Tension:
16 sts and 12 rows measure 10cm (4in) square over patt on 5.00mm (UK 6) hook
IT IS ESSENTIAL TO WORK TO THE STATED TENSION TO ACHIEVE SUCCESS
What you have to do:
Work separate welts and cuffs in rows of twisted treble rib. Pick up stitches from long edge of welt to work main part of body and sleeves. Shape armholes, front opening, sleeves and work shoulder extension at top of sleeves as instructed. Make separate collar, with buttonholes, in twisted treble rib and sew to neck edge and opening, overlapping at centre front.

Instructions

BACK:
Welt:
With 4.00mm (UK 8) hook make 14ch.
Foundation row: (RS) 1tr in 4th ch from hook, 1tr in each ch to end, turn. 12 sts.
Rib row: 2ch (counts as first st), miss st at base of ch, 1twtf in each st, working last twtf in top of turning ch, turn.* Rep last row 52[54:58:60] times more. Fasten off.

Main part:
With 5.00mm (UK 6) hook and RS of welt facing, join yarn at right of one long edge.
1st foundation row: (RS) 1ch (counts as first dc), 3dc in side edge of every 2 rows to end[last 2 rows:last 2 rows:end], 2nd size only: 4dc in side edge of last 2 rows; 3rd size only: 2dc in side edge of last 2 rows, turn. 82[86:90:94] sts.

Abbreviations:

beg = beginning
ch = chain(s)
cm = centimetre(s)
cont = continue
dc = double crochet
dec = decrease(d)
foll = follow(s)(ing)
htr = half treble
inc = increase
patt = pattern
rep = repeat
RS = right side
sp = space
st(s) = stitch(es)
tog = together
tr = treble
twtb = twisted treble back as foll: yrh, insert hook from back in space before next st (between 2 sts) then bring it out from front to back through top of st to be worked, under 2 loops, yrh and draw a loop through, complete tr in usual way
twtf = twisted treble front as foll: yrh, insert hook from front in space before next st (between 2 sts) then bring it out from back to front through top of st to be worked, under 2 loops, yrh and draw a loop through, complete tr in usual way
WS = wrong side
yrh = yarn round hook

2nd foundation row: 2ch (counts as first st), miss st at base of ch, 1tr in each st to end, ending 1htr in 1ch, turn.
Cont in twisted tr patt as foll:
1st patt row: (RS) 2ch (counts as first st), miss st at base of ch, 1twtf in each st, ending 1htr in 2nd of 2ch, turn.
2nd patt row: 2ch, miss st at base of ch, 1twtb in each st, ending 1htr in 2nd of 2ch, turn. Rep last 2 rows until Back measures 40[42:42:44]cm (15¾[16½:16½:17¼]in) in all, ending with a WS row. Fasten off.

Shape armholes:
1st dec row: With RS facing, leave first 4 sts and rejoin yarn to 5th st, 2ch (does NOT count as a st), patt to last 6 sts, (1twtf in next st tog with 1htr in foll st), turn leaving 4 sts unworked. 72[76:80:84] sts.
2nd dec row: 2ch, miss 2 sts tog, patt to last 2twtf, (1twtb in next st tog with 1htr in foll st), turn leaving 2ch unworked. (1 st dec at each end.)**
3rd dec row: 2ch, miss 2 sts tog, patt to last 2twtb, (1twtf in next st tog with 1htr in foll st), turn leaving 2ch unworked. (1 st dec at each end.) Rep 2nd and 3rd dec rows 1[2:2:3] times more.
1st and 3rd sizes only:
Work 2nd dec row again.

All sizes:
62[64:66:68] sts and 6[7:8:9] shaping rows complete.
Next row: Patt to end, working last htr in last twtb or twtf, turn leaving 2ch unworked.
Work 11[10:11:10] more rows in twisted tr patt, ending with a 2nd patt row. 18[18:20:20] rows in all from beg of armhole shaping. Fasten off.

FRONT:
Work as given for Back to **.70[74:78:82] sts.
Divide for neck:
First side: 1st row: 2ch, miss 2 sts tog, patt 28[30:32:34] sts, turn and cont on these sts only. Keeping neck edge straight, dec 1 st at armhole edge (in same way as given for Back shaping) on next 3[4:5:6] rows. 25[26:27:28] sts.
Work 4[3:3:2] rows straight, ending with a WS[WS:RS:RS] row. Keeping armhole edge straight, dec 1 st at neck edge on next 7[7:8:8] rows, ending with a RS row. 18[19:19:20] sts. Work 1 row straight. 18[18:20:20] rows in all from beg of armhole shaping. Fasten off.
Second side: With RS of Front facing, leave 12 sts unworked at centre front, rejoin yarn to next st, 2ch, patt to last 2twtb, (1twtf in next st tog with 1htr in

foll st), turn leaving 2ch unworked. Complete to match first side, reversing shaping.

LEFT SLEEVE:
Cuff:
Work as given for Back welt to *. Rep rib row 24[24:26:26] times more. Fasten off.

Main part:
With 5.00mm (UK 6) hook and RS of cuff facing, join yarn at right of one long edge.

1st foundation row: (RS) 1ch (counts as first dc), 3dc in side edge of every 2 rows to end[end:last 2 rows:last 2 rows], 3rd and 4th sizes only: 2dc in side edge of last 2 rows, turn. 40[40:42:42] sts.

2nd foundation row: Work as given for Back.

Shape sleeve:
1st inc row: As 1st patt row of Back.

2nd inc row: 2ch, miss st at base of ch, 2twtb in next twtf, patt to last 2 sts, 2twtb in last twtf, 1htr in 2nd of 2ch, turn.

3rd and 4th inc rows: Patt as set.

5th inc row: 2ch, miss st at base of ch, 2twtf in next twtb, patt to last 2 sts, 2twtf in next twtb, 1htr in 2nd of 2ch, turn.

6th inc row: Patt as set. 44[44:46:46] sts.
Rep last 6 rows 5 times more.

3rd and 4th sizes only:
Work 1st and 2nd inc rows again.

All sizes:
64[64:68:68] sts.
Cont in patt until Sleeve measures 46[47.5:49:50.5]cm (18[18¾:19¼:20]in) in all, ending with a WS row. Fasten off.

Shape sleeve top:
Work 1st–3rd dec rows as given for Back armhole shaping. Rep 2nd and 3rd dec rows 7[7:8:8] times more, then work 2nd dec row again. 20 sts and 18[18:20:20] rows in all from beg of sleeve top shaping.

Shoulder extension:
Work 14 rows in twisted tr rib as given for Back welt, ending with a WS row.***

Shape neck:
Next row: 2ch, patt 7 sts, (1twtf in next st tog with 1htr in foll st), turn leaving 10 sts unworked.

Next row: 2ch (does NOT count as a st), miss 2 sts tog, patt to end, turn. 8 sts. Work a further 8[8:10:10] rows in rib. Fasten off.

RIGHT SLEEVE:
Work as given for Left sleeve to ***. Fasten off.

Shape neck:
Next row: Leave 10 sts unworked, rejoin yarn to next st, 2ch, patt to end, turn.

Next row: Patt to last 2twtf, (1twtf in next st tog with 1htr in foll st), turn. 8 sts. Work further 8[8:10:10] rows in rib. Fasten off.

Making up

Join top edges of two shoulder extensions. Placing this seam at centre back, join side edges of shoulder extensions to top edge of back. Join opposite side edges of first sections of shoulder extensions to top edges of front. Join sleeve edges to armholes, matching row for row. Join side and sleeve seams.

Collar:
With 4.00mm (UK 8) hook make 15ch. Work foundation row and rib row as given for Back welt. 13 sts. Cont in twisted tr rib as foll:

Buttonhole row: 2ch, miss st at base of ch, patt 4 sts, twtf2tog over next 2 sts, 1ch, patt 5 sts, 1htr in 2nd of 2ch, turn.

Next row: Patt to end, working 1htr in 1ch sp, turn.

Next row: Patt to end, working 1twtf in htr, turn.

Next row: Patt to end.
Rep last 4 rows twice more. Cont in patt until collar fits all round neck edge. Do not fasten off. With buttonholes at left front, sew lower edge of collar to sts at centre front neck, then one long edge of collar all around neck edge, stretching slightly to fit (adjust length as required before fastening off). Sew end of collar at centre front, behind buttonholes. Sew on buttons to match buttonholes.

Flower-square cardigan

Panels of flower squares make a delightful design on this cropped cardigan.

This short V-neck cardigan with three-quarter sleeves is worked in ridged trebles and has panels of flower motifs set into the front and back.

The Yarn

Debbie Bliss Cashmerino DK (approx. 110m/120 yards per 50g/1¾oz ball) is a blend of 55% merino wool, 33% microfibre and 12% cashmere. It produces an extremely soft and luxurious fabric that can be machine washed at a low temperature. There is a fantastic range of contemporary colours to choose from.

GETTING STARTED

Simple stitches and shaping, plus diagram to help assemble panels of motifs.

Size:

To fit bust: 81[86:91:96]cm (32[34:36:38]in)
Actual size: 91[96:100:105]cm (36[38:39½:41½]in)
Length: 43[43:46:47]cm (17[17:18:18½]in)
Sleeve seam: 34[34:36:36]cm (13½[13½:14:14]in)
Note: *Figures in square brackets [ ] refer to larger sizes; where there is only one set of figures, it applies to all sizes*

How much yarn:

7[8:8:9] x 50g (1¾oz) balls of Debbie Bliss Cashmerino DK in colour A – Pale Green (shade 29)
1 ball in each of colour B – Raspberry Pink (shade 27) and C – Purple (shade 32)

Hooks:

3.50mm (UK 9) crochet hook
4.00mm (UK 8) crochet hook

Additional item:

3 medium buttons

Tension:

1 flower square measures 9.5cm (3¾in) square; 18 sts and 9 rows measure 10cm (4in) square over ridged tr on 4.00mm (UK 8) hook
IT IS ESSENTIAL TO WORK TO THE STATED TENSION TO ACHIEVE SUCCESS

What you have to do:

First make 16 flower squares and two side panels in ridged trebles; join together to form lower section of cardigan. Continue working in main colour and ridged trebles only, dividing for armholes and shaping as instructed. Work rounds of striped double crochet for border around cuffs and outer edges.

 Instructions

BODY:

Flower square: (make 16)

With 4.00mm (UK 8) hook and B, make 8ch, join with a ss in first ch to form a ring.

1st round: 2ch, work into ring tr3tog, (2ch, tr4tog) 7 times, 2ch, join with a ss in top of tr3tog. 8 petals. Fasten off.

2nd round: Join A to any 2ch sp, 3ch (counts as first tr),

3tr in same sp, (4tr in next 2ch sp, 4ch, 4tr in foll 2ch sp) 3 times, 4tr in last 2ch sp, 4ch, join with a ss in 3rd of 3ch.

3rd round: 3ch, 1tr in each of next 7tr, *(2tr, 3ch, 2tr) in 4ch sp, 1tr in each of next 8tr, rep from * twice more, (2tr, 3ch, 2tr) in last 4ch sp, join with a ss in 3rd of 3ch. Fasten off.

4th round: Join C to any 3ch corner sp, 1ch (counts as

Abbreviations:

beg = beginning
ch = chain(s)
cm = centimetre(s)
cont = continue
dc = double crochet
dc2tog = (insert hook into next st and draw a loop through) twice, yrh and draw through all 3 loops
dec = decrease(d)
foll = follows
inc = increase
patt = pattern
rep = repeat
RS = right side
sp = space
ss = slip stitch
st(s) = stitch(es)
tr = treble
trb = treble in back loop only
trf = treble in front loop only
tr(2)(3)(4)tog = working into back loops on RS rows and front loops on WS rows, work 1tr into each of next 2(3)(4) sts leaving last loop of each on hook, yrh and draw through all 3(4)(5) loops
WS = wrong side
yrh = yarn round hook

first dc), 1dc in same sp, *1dc in each of next 12tr, (2dc, 1ch, 2dc) in 3ch sp, rep from * twice more, 1dc in each of next 12tr, 2dc in last 3ch sp, 1ch, join with a ss in first ch. 16dc on each side of square, plus 1ch at each corner. Fasten off.

Side panel: (make 2)
With 4.00mm (UK 8) hook and A, make 16[20:24:28]ch.
Foundation row: 1tr in 4th ch from hook, 1tr in each ch to end, turn. 14[18:22:26] sts.
1st row: (WS) 3ch (counts as first tr), miss st at base of ch, 1trf in each st, ending 1tr in 3rd of 3ch, turn.
2nd row: 3ch, miss st at base of ch, 1trb in each st, ending 1tr in 3rd of 3ch, turn. These 2 rows form ridged tr patt. Cont in rows of ridged tr as set until 16 rows in all have been completed, ending with a WS row. Fasten off.
Join 16 squares and 2 side panels as shown in diagram, sewing through back loops of motifs and making sure side panels are right way up.
With 4.00mm (UK 8) hook and RS facing, join A to back loop of first dc at top right of panel (marked 'x' on diagram) and cont as foll:
1st row: 2ch (does not count as a st), 1trb in each of next 15dc, *1tr in seam between squares, 1trb in each of next 16dc *, 1tr in seam, 1trb in each of 14[18:22:26]tr of side panel, 1tr in seam, 1trb in each of 16dc, rep from * to * 3 times, 1tr in seam, 1trb in each of 14[18:22:26]tr, rep from * to * once, 1tr in seam, 1trb in each of next 14dc, tr2tog

over last 2dc, turn 163[171:179:187] sts.
2nd row: 2ch, miss tr2tog, 1trf in each st, ending tr2tog over last 2tr and omitting 2ch, turn. 1 st dec at each end of row.
3rd and 4th sizes only:
3rd row: 2ch, miss tr2tog, 1trb in each st, ending tr2tog over last 2tr, turn. 1 st dec at each end of row.
4th row: As 2nd row.
All sizes:
161[169:173:181] sts.

Divide for armholes:
Right front section:
Cont in ridged tr throughout as foll:
1st row: (RS) 2ch, miss tr2tog, work 31[33:33:35]trb as set, tr2tog, turn. 32[34:34:36] sts.
2nd row: 2ch, miss tr2tog, patt to last 2tr, tr2tog, turn. 1 st dec at each end of row. 30[32:32:34] sts.
Rep last row 3[4:3:4] times more. 24[24:26:26] sts.
Dec 1 st at neck edge on next 7[7:8:8] rows. 17[17:18:18] sts. Cont without shaping until Right front section measures 19[19:20:21]cm (7½[7½:8:8¼]in) from beg of armhole. Fasten off.

Back section:
With RS facing, leave 10tr unworked at right armhole and join A to next tr, cont as foll:
1st row: 2ch, work 70[74:78:82]trb as set, tr2tog, turn. 71[75:79:83] sts.
2nd row: 2ch, miss tr2tog, patt to last 2tr, tr2tog, turn.
Rep last row 2[4:4:6] times more. 65[65:69:69] sts. Cont without shaping until armholes measure 1 row less than Right front.

Shape back neck:
Next row: 3ch, miss st at base of ch, work 15[15:16:16] sts as set, tr2tog over next 2tr. 17[17:18:18] sts. Fasten off. Leaving 29[29:31:31] sts unworked at centre back, rejoin yarn to next tr, 2ch, miss st at base of ch, work 16[16:17:17] sts as set, 1tr in 3rd of 3ch. 17[17:18:18] sts. Fasten off.

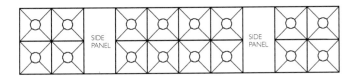

Left front section:

With RS facing, leave 10tr unworked at left armhole and join A to next tr, cont as foll:

1st row: 2ch, work 31[33:33:35]trb as set, tr2tog, turn. 32[34:34:36] sts.

Rep 2nd row as given for Right front section 4[5:4:5] times in all. 24[24:26:26] sts.

Dec 1 st at neck edge on next 7[7:8:8] rows. 17[17:18:18] sts. Cont without shaping until armhole measures same as Right front section. Fasten off.

SLEEVES: (make 2)

With 4.00mm (UK 8) hook and A, make 44[46:48:50] ch. Work foundation row as given for Side panel. 42[44:46:48] sts. Cont in ridged tr throughout, work 1 row.

Shape sleeve:

Inc row: 3ch, 1tr as set in st at base of ch, patt as set, ending 2tr in 3rd of 3ch, turn.

Work 2 rows straight. Rep last 3 rows 7 times more. 58[60:62:64] sts.

Cont without shaping until Sleeve measures 31[31:33:33] cm (12¼[12¼:13:13]in) from beg, ending with a WS row. Fasten off.

Shape top:

1st row: With RS facing, leave first 5tr unworked and rejoin yarn to next tr, 2ch, 1trb in each tr to last 6tr and 3ch, tr2tog over next 2tr, turn leaving 5 sts unworked. 46[48:50:52] sts.

2nd row: 2ch, miss tr2tog, patt as set to last 2tr, tr2tog, turn. 44[46:48:50] sts

Rep last row 8[7:8:9] times more. 28[32:32:32] sts.

Next row: 2ch, miss tr2tog, tr2tog over next 2tr, patt to last 3tr, tr3tog, turn. 24[28:28:28] sts.

Rep last row 1[2:2:2] times more. 20 sts. Fasten off.

CUFFS:

Join sleeve seams.

With 3.50mm (UK 9) hook and RS facing, join A to lower edge at sleeve seam, 1ch, 1dc in base of each ch all around, join with a ss in first ch.

Next round: 1ch, 1dc in each dc, join with a ss in first ch. Cont in rounds of dc, work 1 round B, 2 rounds A and 1 round C. Fasten off.

BAND:

Join shoulder seams.

With 3.50mm (UK 9) hook and RS facing, join A to lower edge at base of seam between back and right side panel and cont as foll:

1st round: 1ch, 1dc in base of each ch along lower edge of side panel, 1dc in back loop of each dc of squares to right front corner, (1dc, 1ch, 1dc) in ch sp at corner, 1dc in back loop of each dc, and 2dc in side edge of each row, up to right back neck corner, dc2tog at corner, 1dc in back loop of each tr across back neck, dc2tog at corner, then cont all around in same way, join with a ss in first ch.

2nd round: 1ch, 1dc in each dc and (1dc, 1ch, 1dc) in ch sp at each corner, join with a ss in first ch. Fasten off A and join in B.

3rd round: As 2nd round, work dc2tog at back neck corners. Fasten off B and join in A.

Buttonhole round: Work as 2nd round to right front corner, (1dc, 1ch, 1dc) at corner, 2dc as set, *4ch, miss 4dc, 1dc in each of next 10dc *, rep from * to * once more, 4ch, miss 4dc, complete as 2nd round.

Next round: Work as 3rd round to first buttonhole, *(dc2tog, inserting hook in same place as last dc and in 4ch sp), 2dc in 4ch sp, (dc2tog, inserting hook in 4ch sp and in next dc), 1dc in same place as last insertion, 1dc in each dc to next buttonhole *, rep from * to * once more, work last buttonhole as set, complete as 3rd round. Fasten off. Join in C and work 1 more round as 2nd round. Fasten off.

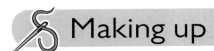

Making up

Sew sleeves into armholes. Sew on buttons to match buttonholes. Press according to directions on ball band.

LOVE cushion

Work a retro vibe with this fabulous letter cushion.

Both in colours and theme, this fabulous cushion is reminiscent of the Seventies. Worked in a Shetland yarn, it has crochet letters appliquéd on to pattern squares that form the front.

The Yarn

Jamieson & Smith Shetland Aran (approx. 90m/98 yards per 50g/1¾oz ball) contains 100% pure Shetland wool. It is a softly spun yarn producing a luxurious, bouncy fabric with crisp stitch definition. There are both traditional and contemporary colours.

GETTING STARTED

 Individual elements are not difficult but they do require concentration and attention to detail.

Size:

Cover fits a 40cm (16in) square pad

How much yarn:

2 x 50g (1¾oz) balls of Jamieson & Smith Shetland Aran in colour A – purple (shade BSS 12)

1 ball in each of four other colours: B – Orange (shade BSS 8); C – Lilac (shade BSS 9); D – Cream (shade BSS 16); E – Mustard (shade BSS 71)

Hook:

4.00mm (UK 8) crochet hook

Additional items:

40cm (16in) square cushion pad

Matching sewing threads and needle

Tension:

15 sts and 8 rows measure 10cm (4in) square over tr on 4.00mm (UK 8) hook

IT IS ESSENTIAL TO WORK TO THE STATED TENSION TO ACHIEVE SUCCESS

What you have to do:

Work front in two panels, each containing a different colour or pattern. Make letters separately. Join front panels and sew on letters, then work striped double crochet edging around entire front. Work back as a giant granny square entirely in one colour.

Instructions

Abbreviations:

alt = alternate
ch = chain(s)
cm = centimetre(s)
cont = continue
dc = double crochet
foll = follows
htr = half treble
patt = pattern
rep = repeat
RS = right side
sp = space
ss = slip stitch
st(s) = stitch(es)
tr = treble
WS = wrong side

FRONT:
Left panel:
With 4.00mm (UK 8) hook and B, make 30ch.

1st row: (RS) 1tr in 4th ch from hook, 1tr in each ch to end, turn.

2nd row: 3ch (counts as first tr), miss st at base of ch, 1tr in each st to end, working last tr in 3rd of 3ch, turn. 28 sts. Rep last row 14 times more. Fasten off. Work in colour block patt as foll, stranding yarn not in use across back of work and working sts over it to conceal:

17th row: (RS) With D, 3ch, miss st at base of ch, work in tr working *2 D, 2 C, rep from * to last 3 sts, 3 D, working last tr in 3rd of 3ch, turn. Fasten off C.

18th row: With D, 1ch (counts as first dc), miss st at base of ch, 1dc in each st to end, working last dc in 3rd of 3ch, turn. Join in E.

19th row: With E, 3ch, miss st at base of ch, work in tr working *2 E, 2 D, rep from * to last 3 sts, 3 E, working last tr in turning ch, turn. Fasten off E.

20th row: As 18th.

21st–35th rows: Rep 17th–20th rows

3 times more, then work 17th–19th rows again. Fasten off.

Right panel:
With 4.00mm (UK 8) hook and E, make 30ch. Joining on new colour on last part of last st in old colour each time, cont as foll:

1st row: (RS) 1tr in 4th ch from hook, 1tr in each ch to end, turn. 28 sts.

2nd row: With D, 2ch (counts as first htr), miss st at base of ch, 1htr in each st to end, working last htr in top of turning ch, turn.

3rd row: With C, 1ch (counts as first dc), 1dc in each st to end, working last dc in turning ch, turn.

4th row: With E, as 3rd.

5th row: With D, as 2nd.

6th row: With C, as 3rd but into FRONT loops only of sts.

7th row: With E, as 2nd.

8th–25th rows: Rep 2nd–7th rows 3 times more.

26th row: As 2nd. Fasten off D and E.

27th row: With C, 3ch (counts as first tr), miss st at base of ch, 1tr in each st to end, working last st in top of turning ch, turn.

28th–41st rows: Rep last row 14 times more. Fasten off.

Letter L:
With 4.00mm (UK 8) hook and A, make 17ch.

1st row: (WS) 1htr in 3rd ch from hook, 1htr in each ch to end, turn. 16 sts.

2nd–4th rows: 2ch (counts as first htr), miss st at base of ch, 1htr in each htrc to end, working last htr in top of turning ch, turn.

5th row: 2ch, miss st at base of ch, 1htr in each of next 5htr, turn. 6htr.

6th–15th rows: Work 10 rows straight in htr on these 6 sts. Fasten off.

Letter O:
With 4.00mm (UK 8) hook and B, make

30ch, join with
a ss in first ch to form a ring.

1st round: 1ch (does not count as a st), 1dc in first ch, (2dc in next ch, 1dc in next ch) to last ch, 1dc in last ch, join with a ss in first dc. 45 sts.

2nd round: With E, 1ch, 1dc in each dc to end, join with a ss in first dc.

3rd round: With D, 1ch, 1dc in each dc to end, join with a ss in first dc.

4th round: As 2nd. Fasten off.

5th round: With B, 1ch, *1dc in each of next 2dc, 2dc in next dc, rep from * to end, join with a ss in first dc. 60 sts.

6th round: With D, *miss 1dc, 5htr in next dc, miss 1dc, ss in next dc, rep from * to end. Fasten off.

Letter V:

With 4.00mm (UK 8) hook and C, make 30ch.

Foundation row: (RS) 1dc in 2nd ch from hook, 1dc in each of next 13ch, 3dc in next ch, 1dc in each of 14ch. Fasten off.

1st round: With RS facing, join E to first dc of foundation row, 1ch, 1dc in first dc, 1dc in each of next 14dc, 3dc in next dc, 1dc in each of next 14dc, 2dc in last dc, working along other side of foundation row, work 2dc in first ch, 1dc in each of 12ch, *insert hook in next ch, yrh and draw loop through *, miss next ch, rep from * to *, yrh and draw through all 3 loops, 1dc in each of 12ch, 2dc in last ch, join with a ss in first ch. Fasten off.

2nd round: With RS facing, join D to second dc of previous round, 1ch (counts as first dc), (1dc in each of next 15dc, 2dc in next dc) twice, 1dc in each of next 2dc, 2dc in next dc, 1dc in each of next 11dc, rep from * to * of 1st round, miss next ch, rep from * to * of 1st round, yrh and draw through all 3 loops, 1dc in each of next 11dc, 2dc in next dc, 1dc in next dc, 1dc in 1ch, join with a ss in first ch. Fasten off.

Letter E:

With 4.00mm (UK 8) hook and A, make 17ch.

1st row: (RS) 1dc in 2nd ch from hook, 1dc in each ch to end, turn. 16 sts.

2nd row: 1ch (counts as first dc), miss st at base of ch, 1dc in each dc to end, turn.

3rd–5th rows: 1ch, miss st at base of ch, 1dc in each dc, 1dc in 1ch, turn.

6th row: 1ch, miss st at base of ch, 1dc in each of next 6dc, turn. 7 sts.

7th–10th rows: Work in dc.

11th row: Make 6ch, 1dc in 2nd ch from hook, 1dc in

each ch and dc to end, turn. 12 sts.

12th–15th rows: Work in dc.

16th–20th rows: As 6th–10th rows.

21st row: Make 10ch, 1dc in 2nd ch from hook, 1dc in each ch and dc to end, turn. 16 sts.

22nd–25th rows: Work in dc. Fasten off.

BACK:

With 4.00mm (UK 8) hook and A, make 5ch, join with a ss into first ch to form a ring.

1st round: 3ch (counts as first tr), 2tr in ring, 3ch, (3tr in ring, 3ch) 3 times, join with a ss in 3rd of 3ch.

2nd round: 3ch, miss st at base of ch, 1tr in each of next 2tr, (2tr, 3ch, 2tr) in 3ch sp, *1tr in each of next 3tr, (2tr, 3ch, 2tr) in 3ch sp, rep from * twice more, join with a ss into 3rd of 3ch.

3rd round: 3ch, miss st at base of ch, 1tr in each of next 4tr, (2tr, 3ch, 2tr) in 3ch sp, *1tr in each of next 7tr, (2tr, 3ch, 2tr) in 3ch sp, rep from * twice more, 1tr in each of last 2tr, join with a ss into 3rd of 3ch.

Cont in this way, working 4tr more on each side of square on every round until 15th round has been completed. Fasten off.

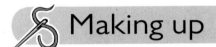

Making up

Sew two front panels together, matching corners and centres exactly. Pin letters in place on squares as shown in picture and slip stitch in position using matching sewing thread.

Front edging:

With 4.00mm (UK 8) hook and RS facing, join E to top right corner, 3dc in first tr, 1dc in each tr along top edge, working 3dc in final tr, 2dc in each row-end down side edge, 3dc in first loop along foundation row, 1dc in each loop along foundation row, working 3dc in final loop, then cont along final edge as foll: 2dc in each tr row-end, 2dc in each htr row-end and 1dc in each dc row-end, join with a ss in first dc. Fasten off. With B and then C, work 2 rounds in dc, working 3dc in each corner st. Fasten off.

With 4.00mm (UK 8) hook, A and with WS facing, crochet front and back together, working dc through corresponding sts of back and front simultaneously and working 3dc in each corner st. After three sides have been joined, insert cushion pad and close fourth side.

Fringed shawl

Silky and soft, this classic shawl makes the perfect light cover-up over a strappy dress.

For the ultimate in luxurious cover-ups, wrap yourself in this soft and silky openwork shawl, which features patterned diamonds and is trimmed on two sides with long tassels.

The Yarn

Sublime Cashmere Merino Silk DK (approx. 116m/126 yards per 50g/1¾oz ball) contains 75% extra-fine merino wool, 20% silk and 5% cashmere to produce a luxurious blend that is extremely soft and silky. It is hand-washable and there is a beautiful palette of understated colours.

GETTING STARTED

Increasing and keeping this openwork pattern correct can be a challenge.

Size:
Approximately 190cm (75in) across top edge x 76cm (30in) long, excluding fringe

How much yarn:
7 x 50g (1¾oz) balls of Sublime Cashmere Merino Silk DK in Smoke Blue (shade 07)

Hook:
4.00mm (UK 8) crochet hook

Tension:
1 diamond measures 5cm (2in) in width x 4cm (1½in) in depth; 4 x 5ch arches measure 9cm (3½in) on 4.00mm (UK 8) hook
IT IS ESSENTIAL TO WORK TO THE STATED TENSION TO ACHIEVE SUCCESS

What you have to do:
Start at lower back point of shawl and make a series of chain arches, increasing at each end of row as instructed. Incorporate patterned diamonds into the shawl as instructed. Finish off top edge with simple double crochet and half treble edging. Add tassels to loops on two sides of shawls.

Instructions

Abbreviations:

ch = chain(s)
cm = centimetre(s)
dc = double crochet
foll = follows
htr = half treble
inc = increase(d)(ing)
patt = pattern
rep = repeat
sp = space
tr = treble(s)
tr2tog = work 2tr leaving last loop of each on hook, yarn round hook and draw through all 3 loops on hook

SHAWL:

With 4.00mm (UK 8) hook make 10ch.

Foundation row: 1dc into 6th ch from hook, 5ch, miss 3ch, 1dc in last ch, 1tr in same ch as last dc, turn.

Next row: 5ch, 1dc in 2ch sp, (5ch, 1dc in next 5ch arch) twice, 2ch, 1tr in same arch as last dc, turn.

Next row: 5ch, 1dc in 2ch sp, (5ch, 1dc in next 5ch arch) 3 times, 2ch, 1tr in same arch as last dc, turn.

Next row: 5ch, 1dc in 2ch sp, (5ch, 1dc in next 5ch arch) 4 times, 2ch, 1tr in same arch as last dc, turn.

Next row: 5ch, 1dc in 2ch sp, (5ch, 1dc in next 5ch arch) 5 times, 2ch, 1tr in same arch as last dc, turn.

Next row: 5ch, 1dc in 2ch sp, (5ch, 1dc in next 5ch arch) 6 times, 2ch, 1tr in same arch as last dc, turn.

Place diamond patt as foll:

1st row: 5ch, 1dc in 2ch sp, (5ch, 1dc in next 5ch arch) 3 times, (tr2tog, 2ch, tr2tog) in next dc, 1dc in next 5ch arch, (5ch, 1dc in next 5ch arch) 3 times, 2ch, 1tr in same arch as last dc, turn.

2nd row: 5ch, 1dc in 2ch sp, (5ch, 1dc in next 5ch arch) 3 times, (tr2tog, 2ch, tr2tog) in next dc, 1dc in next 2ch sp, (tr2tog, 2ch, tr2tog) in next dc, 1dc in next 5ch sp, (5ch, 1dc in next 5ch arch) 3 times, 2ch, 1tr in same arch as last dc, turn.

3rd row: 5ch, 1dc in 2ch sp, (5ch, 1dc in next 5ch arch) 3 times, 5ch, 1dc in next 2ch sp, (tr2tog, 2ch, tr2tog) in next dc, 1dc in next 2ch sp, (5ch, 1dc in next 5ch arch) 4

times, 2ch, 1tr in same arch as last dc, turn.

4th row: 5ch, 1dc in 2ch sp, (5ch, 1dc in next 5ch arch) twice, (tr2tog, 2ch, tr2tog) in next dc, 1dc in next 5ch arch, 5ch, 1dc in next 5ch arch, 5ch, 1dc in next 2ch sp, (5ch, 1dc in next 5ch arch) twice, (tr2tog, 2ch, tr2tog) in next dc, 1dc in next 5ch arch, (5ch, 1dc in next 5ch arch) twice, 2ch, 1tr in same arch as last dc, turn.

5th row: 5ch, 1dc in 5ch sp, (5ch, 1dc in next 5ch arch) twice, (tr2tog, 2ch, tr2tog) in next dc, 1dc in next 2ch sp, (tr2tog, 2ch, tr2tog) in next dc, 1dc in next 5ch arch, (5ch, 1dc in next 5ch arch) 3 times, (tr2tog, 2ch, tr2tog) in next dc, 1dc in next 2ch sp, (tr2tog, 2ch, tr2tog) in next dc, 1dc in next 5ch arch, (5ch, 1dc in next 5ch arch) twice, 2ch, 1tr in same arch as last dc, turn.

6th row: 5ch, 1dc in 2ch sp, (5ch, 1dc in next 5ch arch) twice, 5ch, 1dc in next 2ch sp, (tr2tog, 2ch, tr2tog) in next dc, 1dc in next 2ch sp, (5ch, 1dc in next 5ch arch) 3 times, 5ch, 1dc in next 2ch sp, (tr2tog, 2ch, tr2tog) in next dc, 1dc in next 2ch sp, (5ch, 1dc in next 5ch arch) 3 times, 2ch, 1tr in same arch as last dc, turn.

7th row: 5ch, 1dc in 2ch sp, 5ch, 1dc in next 5ch arch, * (tr2tog, 2ch, tr2tog) in next dc, (1dc in next 5ch arch, 5ch) twice, 1dc in next 2ch sp, (5ch, 1dc in next 5ch arch) twice, rep from * once more, (tr2tog, 2ch, tr2tog) in next dc, 1dc in next 5ch arch, 5ch, 1dc in last 5ch arch, 2ch, 1tr in same arch as last dc, turn.

Cont in patt as now set, inc as before on every row and working diamond patt into inc sts, until shawl measures approximately 74cm (29in) in length, ending with a row that completes the diamonds.

Next row: 5ch, 1dc in 2ch sp, (5ch, 1dc in next 5ch arch or 2ch sp) all along row, 2ch, 1tr in same arch as last dc, turn.

Top edge:
Next row: 1ch (counts as first dc), work in dc evenly along top edge, turn.

Next row: 2ch (counts as first htr), 1htr in each dc to end, turn.

Next row: 1ch, 1dc in each htr to end. Fasten off.

Tassels:
For each tassel cut 6 lengths of yarn each 28cm (11in) long, fold in half and knot tassel in point at lower edge. Work 14 tassels evenly spaced along each side of shawl. Trim as necessary.

Cosy textured beanie

Crochet provides the texture and a knitted rib the elasticity for this neat pull-on hat.

This pull-on hat with a distinctive textured pattern is worked in a soft and cosy yarn. The ribbed band is knitted on afterwards.

GETTING STARTED

★★ *Simple one-row pattern but shaping is required.*

Size:
To fit an average-size adult head

How much yarn:
2 x 50g (1¾oz) balls of Debbie Bliss Cashmerino Aran in ochre (shade 034)

Hook:
5.00mm (UK 6) crochet hook

Additional item:
Pair of 4mm (UK 8) knitting needles

Tension:
17 sts and 22 rows measure 10cm (4in) square over patt on 5.00mm (UK 6) hook
IT IS ESSENTIAL TO WORK TO THE STATED TENSION TO ACHIEVE SUCCESS

What you have to do:
Work main part in rows of textured pattern. Shape crown as directed. Pick up stitches along foundation chain of main part and knit band in twisted rib.

The Yarn
Debbie Bliss Cashmerino Aran (approx. 90m/98 yards per 50g/1¾oz ball) contains 55% merino wool, 33% microfibre and 12% cashmere. This winning combination produces a soft, luxurious fabric, machine-washable at a low temperature. There is a large range of fabulous colours.

Instructions

Abbreviations:

alt = alternate
beg = beginning
ch = chain(s)
cm = centimetre(s)
dc = double crochet
dec = decrease(d)
foll = following
htr = half treble
k = knit
p = purl
patt = pattern
rem = remain(ing)
rep = repeat
RS = right side
ss = slip stitch
st(s) = stitch(es)
tbl = through back
of loop
WS = wrong side
yrh = yarn round hook

BEANIE:
With 5.00mm (UK 6) hook make 104ch.

Foundation row: (WS) Ss into 2nd ch from hook, *1htr into next ch, ss into foll ch, rep from * to end, turn.

Patt row: 1ch (counts as first st), miss first ss, ss into first htr, *1htr into foll ss, ss into next htr, rep from * to end, working last ss into turning ch, turn. 104 sts.
Rep last row to form patt until work measures 10cm (4in) from beg, ending with a WS row.

Shape crown:
1st row: (RS) 1ch (counts as first dc), miss st at base of ch, (insert hook into next st, yrh and draw loop through) 3 times, yrh and draw through all 4 loops on hook (2 sts dec), *1dc into each of next 10 sts, dec 2 sts, rep from * 6 times more, 1dc into each of last 9 sts, turn. 16 sts dec; 88 sts rem.

2nd and every foll alt row: 1ch (counts as first st), *ss into next st, 1htr into foll st, rep from * ending ss into turning ch, turn.

3rd row: I ch, miss st at base of ch, dec 2 sts, *I dc into each of next 8 sts, dec 2 sts, rep from * 6 times more, I dc into each of last 7 sts, turn.
16 sts dec; 72 sts rem.
5th row: I ch, miss st at base of ch, dec 2 sts, *I dc into each of next 6 sts, dec 2 sts, rep from * 6 times more, I dc into each of last 5 sts, turn.
16 sts dec; 56 sts rem.
7th row: I ch, miss st at base of ch, dec 2 sts, *I dc into each of next 4 sts, dec 2 sts, rep from * 6 times more, I dc into each of last 3 sts, turn.
16 sts dec; 40 sts rem.
9th row: I ch, miss st at base of ch, dec 2 sts, *I dc into each of next 2 sts, dec 2 sts, rep from * 6 times more, I dc into last st, turn.
16 sts dec; 24 sts rem.
11th row: I ch, miss st at base of ch, (dec 2 sts) 7 times, I dc into each of last 2 sts, turn. 14 sts dec; 10 sts rem.
12th row: I ch, miss st at base of ch, I dc into each st to end. Fasten off.

Band:
With 4mm (UK 8) needles and RS of work facing, pick up and k104 sts along other side of foundation ch, working each st into rem loop of each ch.
Rib row: (KI tbl, pI) to end.
Rep last row 6 times more. Cast off in rib.

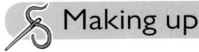 Making up

Join centre back seam from cast-off edge of band to top of crown, take needle through front loop of each st of final row, pull up tightly and fasten off securely.

Tablet case

Make a unique crochet case for your latest bit of computer kit.

Bright and eye-catching, this computer case has floating ring embellishments and a sewn lining, incorporating a pocket and corner stays, in a funky fabric that coordinates with the yarn.

GETTING STARTED

★ ★ *Simple crochet cover but adding sewn lining requires neat sewing skills for a good finish.*

Size:
Approximately 21 x 28cm (8¼ x 11in)

How much yarn:
2 x 50g (1¾oz) balls of Rowan Belle Organic Aran in main colour A – Garnet (shade 216)
1 ball in each of two contrast colours: B – Rose (shade 215); C – Aubergine (shade 201)

Hook:
4.00mm (UK 8) crochet hook

Additional items:
40cm (½ yard) of Amy Butler cotton fabric from Soul Blossoms JOY range – Laurel dots in Cherry AB61
19 x 25cm (7½ x 10in) rectangle of thin wadding
Water-erasable fabric marker
Sewing needle and thread to match main clour

Tension:
17 sts and 9 rows measure 10cm (4in) square over tr on 4.00mm (UK 8) hook
IT IS ESSENTIAL TO WORK TO THE STATED TENSION TO ACHIEVE SUCCESS

What you have to do:
Work rectangle of crochet fabric in trebles for cover. Work four floating ring embellishments directly onto front of cover. Sew fabric lining with pocket and corner stays and sew into cover, adding wadding.

The Yarn
Rowan Belle Organic Aran (approx. 90m/98 yards per 50g/1¾oz ball) is 50% organic wool and 50% organic cotton. This natural yarn is hand-wash only and produces a strong, attractive fabric ideal for craft projects. The good selection of shades team well with Amy Butler fabrics.

Instructions

CASE:
With 4.00mm (UK 8) hook and A, make 72ch.
Foundation row: (RS) 1tr into 4th ch from hook, 1tr into each ch to end, turn. 70 sts.
1st row: 3ch (counts as first tr), miss st at base of ch, 1tr into each st to end, working last tr into 3rd of 3ch, turn. Rep last row 23 times more. Fasten off.

SIDE EDGING:
With 4.00mm (UK 8) hook and RS of work facing, join

7tr around post of adjacent st on same row of case, join with a ss into 3rd of 3ch. 14 sts. Fasten off.

EDGING:

Join C to any tr, 1ch (counts as first dc), 1dc into same st, 1dc into foll st, *2dc into next st, 1dc into foll st, rep from * all round, join with
a ss into first ch. 21 sts. Fasten off.
Rep with other 3 marked positions to give 4 rings.

LOOP FASTENER:

With 4.00mm (UK 8) hook and A, leave a long tail and then make 31ch.
Foundation row: 1dc into 2nd ch from hook, 1dc into each ch to end. Fasten off, leaving a long tail. Using yarn tails, sew loop onto inside back of case, about 2cm (¾in) in from edge (so join will be covered by fabric lining) and positioning ends at 10th and 16th rows.

Abbreviations:

ch = chain
cm = centimetre(s)
dc = double crochet
foll = follow(s)(ing)
rep = repeat
RS = right side
ss = slip stitch
st(s) = stitches
tr = treble
WS = wrong side

A to one side edge of case, 1ch, 2dc into each row end along side edge. Fasten off. Work edging along other side edge in same way.

FLOATING RINGS:

Fold case in half, WS facing and short sides (with edging) matching, and mark positions for rings with pins on front of case. First, count 13 rows up from lower edge to find centre row. From open edge, count 7 sts in and mark with a pin, then rep 3 more times for the positions of next 3 rings.
Note: When working a ring, you will be working first ring onto post of marked st, then having turned case ¾180 degrees, completing second half of ring by working onto post of st adjacent to one just worked. With 4.00mm (UK 8) hook and RS of case facing, join B onto post of first marked st, 3ch (counts as first tr), 6tr onto same post, turn case around through 180 degrees then cont ring by working

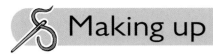

Making up

Cut lining fabric into pieces as foll: 43 × 29cm (17 × 11½in) rectangle for main lining; 30 × 29cm (12 × 11½in) rectangle for pocket and four 13 × 7cm (5 × 2¾in) strips for corner stays.

Make lining and pocket:

Fold pocket piece in half to give a piece 15 × 29cm

(6 × 11½in). Press. Press folded edge over about 1.5cm (⅝in) to create a reinforced edge for pocket opening (fold-over is on RS of pocket). Sew two lines along this folded strip.

Align raw edges of pocket piece with right-hand side of RS of main fabric lining; pin in place. Sew in place along three sides, taking 1cm (⅜in) seam allowance. Fold each corner stay strip in half lengthways with RS facing and sew along open edge, taking 5mm (¼in) seam allowance, to make 4 tubes. Turn each tube RS out and press.

Take two tubes (for middle corner stays) and on each, fold one corner diagonally across to the opposite long edge; press, open out and create a valley fold, ie. push the fabric of the triangle into the tube to create a neat diagonal edge. Sew closed. Now mark off the following on main fabric lining:

Fold fabric in half, short edges together – press (middle crease). With pocket on right, mark off a parallel line 5mm (¼in) to left of middle crease for corner stays placement.

From middle crease, mark off a line 20cm (8in) away down both side edges for outer edges, short sides, of lining. Mark off top and bottom hem on long sides 1.5cm (⅝in) from fabric edge. Press under all outer hemlines. On the left-hand side where you will be placing two corner stays, measuring from each corner created by hemlines, mark off 1cm (⅜in) from corners along hemline at either side. Now position stays so that outer long edge is diagonally across corner, matched up to 1cm (⅜in) marks – make sure the overhang is evenly spread either side – pin in place. Sew to main fabric lining, 1cm (⅜in) from edge.

For the middle corner stays, at top and bottom edge mark off 1cm (⅜in) along hemline to left of middle crease and 1cm (⅜in) from hemline along middle crease.

Top corner stay: With point facing down and shaped end to parallel line to left of middle crease, align top edge with marker on middle crease (other end will overlap pocket). Sew corner stay along line of middle crease. Do the same, in reverse to position the bottom corner stay. Fold over and match up other edge of stays to 1cm (⅜in) marks on hemlines, pin in place. Sew to main fabric lining, 1cm (⅜in) from edge. Carefully fold stays over hem edge, press again. Position wadding centrally on crochet cover, WS facing. Align fabric lining on top, tablet corner stays on left, pocket on right. Tuck in hem edge, pin or tack all around, then hand-sew lining to crochet fabric.

Classic tweed gloves

Crochet a pair of classic gloves in a lovely tweedy yarn.

Worked in a warm tweedy yarn with a felted finish, these gloves are a classic shape and have a turn-back cuff that is knitted in rib for a snug fit.

The Yarn

Rowan Felted Tweed DK (approx. 175m/191 yards per 50g/1¾oz ball) contains 50% merino wool, 25% alpaca and 25% viscose. It produces a soft, warm fabric, machine-washable at a low temperatures. The large range includes plenty of natural shades and colourful heathery ones.

GETTING STARTED

★★ *If you follow the instructions closely, basic fabric and gloves are not complicated.*

Size:
To fit an average-sized woman's hand

How much yarn:
2 x 50g (1¾oz) balls of Rowan Felted Tweed in Paisley (shade 171)

Hook:
3.00mm (UK 11) hook

Additional item:
Pair of 2.75mm (UK 12) knitting needles

Tension:
20 sts and 24 rows measure 10cm (4in) square over dc on 3.00mm (UK 11) hook
IT IS ESSENTIAL TO WORK TO THE STATED TENSION TO ACHIEVE SUCCESS

What you have to do:
Work hand in rows of double crochet, shaping for thumb as directed. Work fingers and thumb in rounds of double crochet as directed. Pick up stitches from wrist edge and knit cuff in single rib.

Instructions

Abbreviations:

alt = alternate
beg = begin
ch = chain(s)
cm = centimetre(s)
cont = continue
dc = double crochet
dc2tog = (insert hook in next st, yrh and draw a loop through) twice, yrh and draw through all 3 loops
dec = decrease
foll = following
inc = increas(e)(s)(ing)
k = knit; **p** = purl
rep = repeat
RS = right side
ss = slip stitch
st(s) = stitch(es)
WS = wrong side
yrh = yarn round hook

GLOVE:

With 3.00mm (UK 11) hook make 36ch loosely and beg at wrist.

1st row: (RS) 1dc in 2nd ch from hook, 1dc in each ch to end, turn.

2nd row: 1ch (counts as first dc), miss dc at base of ch, 1dc in each dc to end, working last dc in 1ch, turn. 36 sts.

Rep last row twice more. 4 rows in all.

Shape thumb:

5th row: 1ch, miss st at base of ch, 1dc in each of next 16 sts, (2dc in next st) twice, 1dc in each of next 16 sts, 1dc in 1ch, turn. 38 sts.

6th row: As 2nd row.

7th row: 1ch, miss st at base of ch, 1dc in each of next 16 sts, 2dc in next st, 1dc in each of next 2 sts, 2dc in next st, 1dc in each of next 16 sts, 1dc in 1ch, turn. 40 sts.

8th row: As 2nd row.

Cont in this way, inc 2 sts (with 2 extra sts between incs) on next and every foll alt row, for a further 8 rows, ending with a WS row. 48 sts; 16 rows in all.

Rep 2nd row 4 times more. 20 rows in all.

Shape thumb hole:

21st row: 1ch, miss st at base of ch, 1dc in each of next 17 sts, 2ch, miss next 12 sts, 1dc in each of next 17 sts, 1dc in 1ch, turn.

22nd row: 1ch, miss st at base of ch, 1dc in each of next 17 sts, 1dc in each of 2ch, 1dc in each of next 17 sts, 1dc in 1ch,

turn. 38 sts.
Rep 2nd row 6 more times. 28 rows in all.

Little finger:
Note: All fingers are worked in rounds. When fastening off each finger, leave a 20cm (8in) tail.

1st round: 1ch, miss st at base of ch, 1dc in each of next 3 sts, 2ch, miss next 30 sts, 1dc in each of next 3 sts, 1dc in 1ch, join with a ss in first ch. 10 sts.

2nd round: 1ch, miss st at base of ch, 1dc in each of next 3 sts, 1dc in each of 2ch, 1dc in each of next 4 sts, join with a ss in first ch.

3rd round: 1ch, miss st at base of ch, 1dc in each st, join with a ss in first ch.
Rep last round 8 times more. 11 rounds in all.

Dec round: 1ch, miss st at base of ch, (dc2tog) 4 times, 1dc in last st, join with a ss in first ch.
Fasten off.

Ring finger:
With RS of work facing, rejoin yarn to base of first of 2ch made on 1st round of Little finger.

1st round: 1ch, miss st at base of ch, 1dc in each of next 4 sts, 2ch, miss next 22 sts, 1dc in each of last 4 sts, 1dc in 2nd of 2ch, join with a ss in first ch. 12 sts.

2nd round: 1ch, miss st at base of ch, 1dc in each of next 4 sts, 1dc in each of next 2ch, 1dc in each of next 5 sts, join with a ss in first ch.
Rep 3rd round of Little finger 12 times. 14 rounds in all.

Dec round: 1ch, miss st at base of ch, (dc2tog) 5 times, 1dc in last st, join with a ss in first ch.
Fasten off.

Middle finger:
With RS of work facing, rejoin yarn to base of first of 2ch made on 1st round of Ring finger.

1st round: 1ch, miss st at base of ch, 1dc in each of next

5 sts, 2ch, miss next 12 sts, 1dc in each of last 5 sts, 1dc in 2nd of 2ch, join with a ss in first ch. 14 sts.

2nd round: 1ch, miss st at base of ch, 1dc in each of next 5 sts, 1dc in each of next 2ch, 1dc in each of next 6 sts, join with a ss in first ch. Rep 3rd round of Little finger 14 times. 16 rounds in all.

Dec round: 1ch, miss st at base of ch, (dc2tog) 6 times, 1dc in last st, join with a ss in first ch.
Fasten off.

Forefinger:
With RS of work facing, rejoin yarn to base of first of 2ch made on 1st round of Middle finger.

1st round: 1ch, miss st at base of ch, 1dc in each of next 12 sts, 1dc in 2nd of 2ch, join with a ss in first ch. 14 sts.
Rep 3rd round of Little finger 14 times. 15 rounds in all.

Dec round: 1ch, miss st at base of ch, (dc2tog) 6 times, 1dc in last st, join with a ss in first ch.
Fasten off.

Thumb:
With RS of work facing, rejoin yarn to base of first of 2ch made on 21st row.

1st round: 1ch, miss st at base of ch, 1dc in each of next 12 sts, 1dc in 2nd of 2ch, join with a ss in first ch. 14 sts.
Rep 3rd round of Little finger 12 times. 13 rounds in all.

Dec round: 1ch, miss st at base of ch, (dc2tog) 6 times, 1dc in last st, join with a ss in first ch.
Fasten off.

Cuff:
With 2.75mm (UK 12) needles and RS of work facing, pick up and k 1 st from base of each of 36ch along wrist edge.

Inc row: *K1, p1, k into next st leaving st on left needle, then p into same st, rep from * to end. 48 sts.

Rib row: *K1, p1, rep from * to end.
Rep rib row until cuff measures 13cm (5in) in all, ending with a WS row. Cast off loosely in rib.

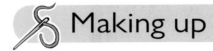

Making up

Turn inside out. At top of thumb and each finger, thread yarn tail into yarn needle and gather up top edge, securing firmly. Join cuff and side seam, reversing seam on cuff to fold back.

Hexagonal throw

Hexagons make an interesting change from traditional granny squares and create a stunning throw.

Worked in an Aran yarn, this sensational throw features multi-colour hexagonal motifs each surrounded by a cream border and pretty picot joining rows.

The Yarn

Debbie Bliss Rialto Aran (approx. 80m/87 yards per 50g/1¾oz ball) contains 100% merino wool. It produces a warm fabric that feels soft and cosy. Machine washable at a low temperature, there are plenty of fabulous shades to choose from.

GETTING STARTED

Hexagons are easy to make with practice but joining requires patience and skill.

Size:

Finished throw measures approximately 100cm (40in) wide (between outer points of hexagons) and 112cm (44in) long (between top and bottom sides of hexagons)

How much yarn:

3 x 50g (1¾oz) balls of Debbie Bliss Rialto Aran in each of four colours: A – Red (shade 18); B – Gold (shade 34); C – Green (shade 10) and D – Beige (shade 01)
2 balls in E – Chocolate (shade 19)
8 balls in F – Off-white (shade 16)

Hook:

5.00mm (UK 6) crochet hook

Tension:

One hexagonal motif measures 14cm (5½in) across from point to point and 12cm (4¾in) across from side to side on 5.00mm (UK 6) hook
IT IS ESSENTIAL TO WORK TO THE STATED TENSION TO ACHIEVE SUCCESS

What you have to do:

Work hexagonal motifs in rounds of trebles in either plain colours or with colour changes as indicated in diagram. Use same colour to work double crochet border featuring half treble picot loops around each motif. Join motifs through picot loops while working.

Instructions

Abbreviations:

ch = chain(s)

cm = centimetre(s)

dc = double crochet

htr = half treble

rep = repeat

sp(s) = space(s)

ss = slip stitch

st(s) = stitch(es)

tog = together

tr = treble

tr2(3)tog = (yrh, insert hook as directed and draw a loop through, yrh and draw through first 2 loops on hook) 2(3) times, yrh and draw through all 3(4) loops on hook

yrh = yarn round hook

BASIC HEXAGON:

With 5.00mm (UK 6) hook and 1st colour, make 8ch, join with a ss into first ch to form a ring.

1st round: 3ch, tr2tog into ring (counts as tr3tog), (3ch, tr3tog into ring) 5 times, 1ch, join with 1htr into top of tr2tog, changing to 2nd colour (if necessary) on last part of st.

2nd round: 3ch, tr2tog into arch formed by htr at end of previous round, *3ch, (tr3tog, 3ch, tr3tog) into next sp, rep from * 4 times more, 3ch, tr3tog into last sp, 1ch, join with 1htr into top of tr2tog.

3rd round: 3ch, tr2tog into arch formed by htr at end of previous round, *3ch, (tr3tog, 3ch, tr3tog) into next sp **, 3ch, tr3tog into next sp, rep from * 4 times more and then from * to ** again, 1ch, join with 1htr into top of tr2tog, changing to 3rd colour (if necessary) on last part of st.

4th round: 3ch (counts as 1tr), 1tr into arch formed by htr at end of previous round, *3tr into next sp, (3tr, 2ch, 3tr) into next sp **, 3tr into next sp, rep from * 4 times more and then from * to ** again, 1tr into next sp, join with a ss into top of 3ch. Fasten off.

Following these instructions and using diagram as a guide to colours, make a total of 46 hexagons.

■ A ■ C ■ E
□ B □ D

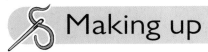

Making up

First hexagon:

1st round: Join F into any corner sp of first hexagon, 1ch (does not count as a st), (2dc into corner sp, 1dc into each of 12tr along one side of hexagon) 6 times, join with a ss into first dc.

2nd round: 1ch, 1dc into st at base of ch, *4ch, 1htr into 4th ch from hook, miss 1dc, 1dc into next dc, (4ch, 1htr into 4th ch from hook, miss next 2dc, 1dc into next dc) 4 times **, rep from * 5 times more, omitting last dc and joining with a ss into first dc. Fasten off.

Second hexagon:

1st round: Work as given for 1st round of First hexagon.

2nd round: Work as given for 2nd round of First hexagon to **, then rep from * 3 times more, 4ch, insert hook from back to front through htr loop on corresponding corner point of First hexagon, yrh and draw a loop through drawing it through loop on hook, 1htr into 4th ch from hook, miss 1dc and work 1dc into next dc on Second hexagon, (4ch, insert hook through next htr loop on First hexagon, yrh and draw a loop through as before, 1htr into 4th ch from hook, miss next 2dc and work 1dc into next dc on Second hexagon) 4 times, 4ch, insert hook through corresponding corner point on First hexagon, yrh and draw loop through as before, 1htr into 4th ch from hook, miss 1dc and work 1dc into next dc on Second hexagon, (4ch, 1htr into 4th ch from hook, miss next 2dc and work 1dc into next dc on Second hexagon) 4 times, omitting last dc and joining with a ss into first dc on Second hexagon. Fasten off.

Using the diagram as a guide, complete First row, joining first 7 hexagons in this way.

Cont to join hexagons in rows, following numerical order of diagram. Note that on subsequent rows hexagons will join on either two or three sides. Where 3 hexagons meet at corner point, work 4ch and then insert hook from front to back through loop of adjacent corner point and then from back to front through loop of opposite corner point as well before working 1htr into 4th ch from hook.

Flared jacket with collar

Buttoned or unbuttoned, this jacket looks stylishly on trend.

With its fabric of double crochet and trebles, collar and three buttons, this neat, slightly flared jacket makes a perfect addition to your wardrobe.

GETTING STARTED

Simple fabric but plenty of shaping and must be worked neatly for the best effect.

Size:

To fit bust: 82–86[92–97:102–107]cm (82–86[36–38:40–42]in)
Actual size: 93[103:113]cm (36½[40½:44½]in)
Length: 61[63:65]cm (24[24¾:25½]in)
Sleeve seam: 31.5cm (12⅜in)
Note: Figures in square brackets [ ] refer to larger sizes; one set of figures only applies to all sizes

How much yarn:

15[16:17] x 50g (1¾oz) balls of Sublime Extra Fine Merino Wool DK in Dark Forest (shade 172)

Hook:

4.00mm (UK 8) crochet hook

Additional item:

3 large buttons

Tension:

18 sts measure 10cm (4in) and 12 rows measure 8cm (3⅛in) over patt on 4.00mm (UK 8) hook
IT IS ESSENTIAL TO WORK TO THE STATED TENSION TO ACHIEVE SUCCESS

What you have to do:

Work pattern in alternate rows of trebles and double crochet throughout. Shape side edges, armholes, neckline, sleeves and collar as directed. Make buttonholes in right front. Work double crochet edging from left to right (crab stitch) around all outer edges to neaten.

The Yarn

Sublime Extra Fine Merino Wool DK (approx. 116m/126 yards per 50g/1¾oz ball) is 100% merino wool. It is a luxuriously smooth yarn that gives clear stitch definition and it is machine-washable at a low temperature. There is a wide palette of fabulous colours.

Instructions

BACK:

With 4.00mm (UK 8) hook make 103[112:121]ch.

1st row: (RS) 1dc in 3rd ch from hook, 1dc in each ch to end, turn. 102[111:120] sts.

2nd row: 2ch (counts as first tr), miss st at base of ch, 1tr in each st, ending 1tr in 2nd of 2ch, turn.

3rd row: 1ch (counts as first dc), miss st at base of ch, 1dc in each st, ending 1dc in 2nd of 2ch, turn.

4th row: 2ch, miss st at base of ch, 1tr in each st, ending 1tr in 1ch, turn. 3rd and 4th rows form patt.

5th row: As 3rd row. **

6th row: (WS) 2ch, miss st at base of ch, tr2tog over next 2 sts, 1tr in each st to last 3 sts, tr2tog over next 2 sts, 1tr in 1ch, turn. 1 st dec at each end. Cont to dec in this way at each end of every foll 6th row 8 times more. 84[93:102] sts. Patt 6 rows straight, ending with a WS row. (60 rows worked in total.)

Shape armholes:

1st row: (RS) Fasten off, miss first

Abbreviations:

alt = alternate
beg = beginning
ch = chain
cm = centimetre(s)
cont = continue
dc = double crochet
dc2tog = (insert hook in next st, yrh and draw loop through) twice, yrh and draw through all 3 loops
dec = decrease(d)
foll = follow(s)(ing)
inc = increase
patt = pattern
rem = remain
rep = repeat
RS = right side
st(s) = stitch(es)
tog = together
tr = treble
tr2tog = (yrh, insert hook in next st and draw through a loop, yrh round hook and draw through first 2 loops on hook) twice, yrh and draw through all 3 loops on hook
WS = wrong side
yrh = yarn round hook

5 sts, rejoin yarn in next st and make 1ch, 1dc in each st to last 5 sts, turn. 74[83:92] sts. Working tr2tog one st in from each end of WS rows and dc2tog one st in from each end of RS rows, dec one st at each end of next 5[7:9] rows. 64[69:74] sts. Patt 20 rows straight, ending with a WS row.

Shape neck:

1st row: (RS) Patt 24[25:26] sts, turn. Working alt tr2tog and dc2tog as before, dec one st in from neck edge on next 4 rows. 20[21:22] sts. Fasten off.
Next row: (RS) Miss centre 16[19:22] sts, rejoin yarn in next st and make 1ch, 1dc in each st to end.
Complete to match first side of neck.

LEFT FRONT:

With 4.00mm (UK 8) hook make 58[62:67] ch. Work as given for Back to **. 57[61:66] sts. ***
6th row: (WS) 2ch, miss st at base of ch, 1tr in each st to last 3 sts, tr2tog over next 2 sts, 1tr in 1ch, turn. 1st dec at side edge. Cont to dec in this way at side edge on every foll 6th row 8 times more. 48[52:57] sts. Patt 6 rows straight, ending with a WS row.

Shape armhole:

1st row: (RS) Fasten off, miss first 5 sts, rejoin yarn in next st and make 1ch,

1dc in each st to end, turn. 43[47:52] sts. Working alt tr2tog and dc2tog as before, dec one st in from armhole edge on next 5[7:9] rows. 38[40:43] sts. Patt 16 rows straight, ending with a WS row.

Shape neck:

1st row: (RS) Patt 24[25:26] sts, turn. Working alt tr2tog and dc2tog as before, dec one st in from neck edge on next 4 rows. 20[21:22] sts. Patt 4 rows straight. Fasten off.

RIGHT FRONT:

Work as given for Left front to ***.
6th row: (WS) 2ch, miss st at base of ch, tr2tog over next 2 sts, 1tr in each st to end, turn. 1st dec at side edge. Cont to dec in this way at side edge on every foll 6th row 8 times more. 48[52:57] sts. Patt 6 rows straight, ending with a WS row.

Shape armhole:

1st row: (RS) Patt to last 5 sts, turn. 43[47:52] sts.
Dec as before one st in from armhole edge on next 1[3:5] rows.
1st buttonhole row: (RS) Marking this row, patt 6 sts, 4ch, miss next 4 sts, patt to last 3 sts, dc2tog over next 2 sts, 1dc in 2nd of 2ch, turn. Working 1tr in each of

4ch on next row, cont to dec at armhole edge on next 3 rows. 38[40:43] sts. Keeping armhole edge straight, make 2nd buttonhole 8 rows from 1st buttonhole row (marker) and 3rd buttonhole 8 rows from 2nd. Patt 3 rows straight, ending with a WS row.

Shape neck:

1st row: (RS) Fasten off, miss 14[15:17] sts, rejoin yarn in next st and make 1ch, 1dc in each st to end, turn. Complete to match Left front.

SLEEVES: (make 2)

With 4.00mm (UK 8) hook make 49[51:53]ch. Work as given for 1st–3rd rows of Back. 48[50:52] sts.

Dec row: (WS) 2ch, miss st at base of ch, tr2tog over next 2 sts, 1tr in each st to last 3 sts, tr2tog over next 2 sts, 1tr in 1ch, turn. 46[48:50] sts. Patt 3 rows straight, then rep dec row. 44[46:48] sts. Patt 3[7:5] rows straight.

Inc row: (WS) 2ch, miss st at base of ch, 2tr in next st, 1tr in each st to last 2 sts, 2tr in next st, 1tr in 1ch, turn. 46[48:50] sts.

Cont to inc one st at each end of every foll 4th[3rd:3rd] row 8[9:10] times. 62[66:70] sts.

Patt 2[3:2] rows, ending with a WS row.

(46 rows worked in total.)

Shape top:

1st row: (RS) Fasten off, miss first 5 sts, rejoin yarn in next st and make 1ch, 1dc in each st to last 5 sts, turn. 52[56:60] sts.

Working tr2tog, dec one st in from each end of every WS row 8 times. 36[40:44] sts. Dec one st at each end of next 4 rows. 28[32:36] sts. Work (dc2tog) twice, one st in from each end of next row and (tr2tog) twice, one st in from each end of foll row. 20[24:28] sts. Fasten off.

COLLAR:

Join shoulder seams as foll: with RS tog, work 1dc in each pair of sts of shoulders.

With 4.00mm (UK 8) hook and WS facing, join yarn in 9th[10th:11th] st of neck edge of left front, 1ch, 1dc in each of next 5[5:6] sts, 13dc up left front neck, 7dc down left back neck, 16[19:22]dc across back neck, 7dc up right back neck, 13dc down right front neck and 6[6:7]dc in neck edge of right front. 68[71:76] sts.

1st inc row: 2ch, miss st at base of ch, 1tr in each of next 28[28:32] sts, 2tr in next st, (1tr in each of next 2 sts, 2tr in next st) 3[4:3] times, 1tr in each of next 29[29:33] sts, turn. 72[76:80] sts.

Patt 3 rows straight.

2nd inc row: 2ch, miss st at base of ch, 1tr in each of next 2 sts, 2tr in next st, (1tr in each of next 3 sts, 2tr in next st) 6 times, 1tr in each of next 16[20:24] sts, (2tr in next st, 1tr in each of next 3 sts) 7 times, turn. 86[90:94] sts. Patt 3 rows straight.

3rd inc row: 2ch, miss st at base of ch, 1tr in each of next 3 sts, 2tr in next st, (1tr in each of next 4 sts, 2tr in next st) 6 times, 1tr in each of next 16[20:24] sts, (2tr in next st, 1tr in each of next 4 sts) 7 times. 100[104:108] sts. Patt 2 rows straight.

1st dec row: 2ch, miss st at base of ch, dc2tog over next 2 sts, 1dc in each st to last 3 sts, dc2tog over next 2 sts, 1dc in top of turning ch, turn.

2nd dec row: 3ch, miss st at base of ch, tr2tog over next 2 sts, 1tr in each st to last 3 sts, tr2tog over next 2 sts, 1tr in 2nd of 2ch, turn. Rep last 2 rows once more. Fasten off.

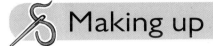

Making up

Press according to directions on ball band. Sew in sleeves. Join side and sleeve seams.

Edging:

With 4.00mm (UK 8) hook and RS facing, start at join of collar on left front and working 2dc in each corner, work 1 row of dc around fronts and lower edge, ending at join of collar on right front. Do not turn but work 1 row of dc from left to right (crab st) along previous row. Fasten off.

With upper side of collar facing, work 2 rows dc around collar in same way. Starting at sleeve seam, edge each sleeve in same way. Sew on buttons.

Inca-style hat

Take your style tips from the mountains of Peru with this take on a classic Inca hat.

Crocheted in a cosy yarn, this Inca-style hat is worked mainly in rounds with bands of coloured motifs. The ear flaps and centre of the crown are trimmed with distinctive plaits, each finished with a tassel.

GETTING STARTED

★★★ *The techniques involved in working these patterns are complicated and require some practice.*

Size:
To fit an average-size adult woman's head

How much yarn:
1 x 50g (1¾oz) ball of Jamieson & Smith Shetland Aran in each of five colours: A – Orange (shade 8); B – Purple (shade 9); C – Soft Turquoise (shade 1); D – Mustard (shade 72) and E – White (shade 16)

Hook:
4.00mm (UK 8) crochet hook

Tension:
14 sts and 8 rows measure 10cm (4in) square over tr on 4.00mm (UK 8) hook
IT IS ESSENTIAL TO WORK TO THE STATED TENSION TO ACHIEVE SUCCESS

What you have to do:
Work crown and sides of hat in rounds of trebles and bands of coloured patterns as instructed. Always join in new colour on last part of stitch in old colour. Crochet over top of colour not in use. Work ear flaps in rows, attaching ends of rows to hat. Work edging mainly in half trebles. Decorate ear flaps and centre of crown with plaits trimmed with tassels.

The Yarn
Jamieson & Smith Shetland Aran (approx. 90m/98 yards per 50g/1¾oz ball) contains 100% Shetland wool. It makes a luxurious and bouncy fabric with crisp stitch definition and provides natural warmth and insulation during colder weather. There is plenty of colour choice.

Instructions

Abbreviations:

ch = chain(s)
cm = centimetre(s)
cont = continue
dc = double crochet
dtr = double treble
foll = follows
htr = half treble
patt(s) = pattern(s)
rep = repeat
RS = right side
sp(s) = space(s)
ss = slip stitch
st(s) = stitch(es)
tr = treble
WS = wrong side

HAT:
Crown:

Make a foundation loop as foll: wind A ten times around index finger of your left hand and roll off wrapped loop carefully.

1st round: Insert hook in loop and work 1ch over strands, now work 12dc in loop, join with a ss in first dc.

2nd round: 3ch (counts as first tr), 1tr in st at base of ch, 2tr in each st to end, join with a ss in 3rd of 3ch. 24 sts.
Now cont in tr and colour patts as foll, noting that new colour should always be

used to work last part of st in old colour. Colour not in use should be laid loosely across top of tr of previous round and enclosed within each tr as it is worked.

3rd round: With A, 3ch, miss st at base of ch, 2tr in next st, 1tr in next st, with B, 1tr in next st, *1tr A in next st, 2tr A in next st, 1tr A in next st, 1tr B in next st, rep from * to end, join with a ss in 3rd of 3ch. 30 sts.

4th round: With B, 3ch, miss st at base of ch, *1trA in each of next 2 sts, with B, 2tr in next st, 1tr in next st, 2tr in next st, rep from * to last 4 sts, 1trA in each of next 2 sts, with B, 2tr in next st, 1tr in last st, 1tr in st at base of 3ch, join with a ss in 3rd of 3ch. 42 sts. Cut off A and B.

5th round: Join C to same place as ss, 3ch, 1tr in st at base of ch, *1tr in each of next 2tr, 2tr in next tr, 1tr in each of next 3tr, 2tr in next tr, rep from * to last 6 sts, 1tr in each of next 2 sts, 2tr in next tr, 1tr in each of last 3 sts, join with a ss in 3rd of 3ch. 54 sts. Cut off C.

6th round: Join D in same place as last ss, 3ch, miss st at base of ch, 1tr in next st, *with E, 1tr in each of next 2 sts, with D, 1tr in each of next 3 sts, with E, 2tr in next st, with D, 1tr in each of next 3 sts, rep from * to last 7 sts, with E, 1tr in each of next 2 sts, with D, 1tr in each of next 3 sts, with E, 2tr in next st, with D, 1tr in last st, with E, join with a ss in 3rd of 3ch. 60 sts.

7th round: With E, 3ch, miss st at base of ch, 1tr in next st, *with D, 2tr in next st, 1tr in next st, with E, 1tr in each of next 3 sts, rep from * to last 3 sts, with D, 2tr in next st, 1tr in next st, with E, 1tr in last st, with D, join with a ss in 3rd of 3ch. 72 sts.

8th round: With D 3ch, miss st at base of ch, 1tr in next st, *with E, 1tr in next st, 2tr in next st, 1tr in next st, with D, 1tr in each of next 3 sts, rep from * to last 4 sts, with E, 1tr in next st, 2tr in next st, 1tr in next st, with D, 1tr in last st, join with a ss in 3rd of 3ch. 84 sts. Cut off D and E.

9th round: Join C in same place as ss, 3ch, 1tr in st at base of ch, 1tr in each of next 20 sts, *2tr in next st, 1tr in each of next 20 sts, rep from * to end, join with a ss in 3rd of 3ch. 88 sts. Cut off C.

Sides:

10th round: Join A to same place as ss, 3ch, miss st at base of ch, 1tr in next st, with B, 1tr in each of next 6 sts, *with A, 1tr in each of next 2 sts, with B, 1tr in each of next 6 sts, rep from * to end, changing to A to join with a ss in 3rd of 3ch.

11th round: With A, 3ch, miss st at base of ch, 1tr in each of next 2 sts, *with B, 1tr in each of next 4 sts, with A, 1tr in each of next 4 sts, rep from * to last 5 sts, with B, 1tr in each of next 4 sts, with A, 1tr in last st, join with a ss in 3rd of 3ch.

12th round: With A, 3ch, miss st at base of ch, 1tr in each of next 3 sts, with B, 1tr in each of next 2 sts, *with A, 1tr in each of next 6 sts, with B, 1tr in each of next 2 sts, rep from * to last 2 sts, with A, 1tr in each of last 2 sts, changing to C to join with a ss in 3rd of 3ch. Cut off B.

13th round: With C, 3ch, miss st at base of ch, 1tr in next st, with A, 1tr in each of next 6 sts, *with C, 1tr in each of next 2 sts, with A, 1tr in each of next 6 sts, rep from * to end, changing to C to join with a ss in 3rd of 3ch.

14th round: With C, 3ch, miss st at base of ch, 1tr in each of next 2 sts, with A, 1tr in each of next 4 sts, *with C, 1tr in each of next 4 sts, with A, 1tr in each of next 4 sts, rep from * to last st, with C, 1tr in last st, join with a ss in 3rd of 3ch.

15th round: With C, 3ch, miss st at base of ch, 1tr in each of next 3 sts, with A, 1tr in each of next 2 sts, *with C, 1tr in each of next 6 sts, with A, 1tr in each of next 2 sts, rep from * to last 2 sts, with C, 1tr in each of last 2 sts, join with a ss in 3rd of 3ch. Cut off A.

16th round: With C, 3ch, miss st at base of ch, 1tr into each st to end, join with a ss in 3rd of 3ch. Fasten off.

Note: Joins of rounds are at centre back of hat.

Ear flaps:

Mark 21st tr to right of join in last round, and 15th tr to left.

With 4.00mm (UK 8) hook and RS of work facing, join D to first marked st and work as foll:

1st row: Ss in same st, miss 2tr, 5tr in next tr, miss 2tr, ss in next tr, 3ch, miss 1tr, ss in next tr of 16th round, turn.

2nd row: With D, miss first ss, 1tr in next ss, *with E, 2tr in next tr, with D, 2tr in next tr, rep from * once more, with E, 2tr in last tr, with D, 2tr in ss, miss 1tr of 16th round, with E, ss in next tr, 3ch, miss next tr of 16th round, ss in next tr, turn.

3rd row: With E, 1tr in first tr, 2tr in next tr, *with D, 1tr in each of next 2tr, with E, 2tr in each of next 2tr, rep from * once more, with D, 1tr in each of next 2tr, with E, 2tr in next tr, 2tr in 3rd of 3ch, miss 1tr of 16th round, ss in next tr, turn.

4th row: With E, ss across first 6 sts, with D, 1dc in each of next 2 sts, 1htr in next st, 1tr in next st, with E, 1tr in each of next 2 sts, with D, 1tr in next st, 1htr in next st, 1dc in each of next 2 sts, ss in next st. Fasten off.

Join D to second marked st and work other ear flap in same way.

Edging:

With 4.00mm (UK 8) hook, B and RS of work facing, start at centre back and work around outer edge as foll: 2ch, 1htr in each st to centre 2 sts in E of ear flaps, 1tr and 2dtr in next st, 2dtr and 1tr in next st, cont in htr, working centre 2 sts of other ear flap in same way, join with a ss in 2nd of 2ch. Fasten off.

Plaits:

Cut 15 x 60-cm (24-in) lengths of B and divide into three bundles of five lengths. Use crochet hook to pull each bundle through one of the sts at point of one ear flap to give 30-cm (12-in) lengths. Pull lengths so that ends are level, then plait evenly and firmly. Tie off 5cm (2in) before end and trim tail into a tassel. Repeat to make a plait on other ear flap.

Tassel:

Wind A, C, D and E around a 15cm (6in)-wide book or piece of card about 8 times for each colour and cut off. Cut 9 x 40cm (16in) lengths of B and slide them under mixed colour yarns on book and level up ends so that hank lies half way along threads in B.

Slide hank off book and tie together tightly close to threads in B. Cut through and trim ends to make a tassel. Plait threads in B, then feed plait through foundation ring and sew securely to WS of hat.

Big-collar cardigan

This is a light yet cosy cardigan; crochet it in russet shades and it's perfect for an autumn day.

Its large collar, beautiful brushed yarn and pretty openwork pattern are the main features of this jacket. The fronts wrap over and fasten on one side with a row of buttons and loops.

The Yarn

Rowan Kidsilk Aura (approx. 75m/82 yards per 25g/1oz ball) is a luxurious blend of 75% kid mohair and 25% silk. Hand-wash only, the yarn is in a good range of classic colours.

GETTING STARTED

★★★ *Working in brushed yarn and keeping openwork pattern correct is a challenge even if experienced.*

Size:
To fit bust: 76–81[86–91:97–102]cm
(30–32[34–36:38–40]in)
Actual size: 91[101:110]cm (36[39¾:43¼]in)
Length: 61cm (24in)
Sleeve seam: 42[42:44]cm (16½[16½:17¼]in)
Note: Figures in square brackets [ ] refer to larger sizes; where there is only one set of figures, it applies to all sizes
How much yarn:
23[25:27] x 25g (1oz) balls of Rowan Kidsilk Aura in Terracotta (shade 772)

Hook:
3.50mm (UK 9) crochet hook
Additional items:
4 buttons, 1 snap fastener
Tension:
20 sts (2 patt repeats) measure 9.5cm (3¾in) and 8 rows measure 9cm (3½in) over patt on 3.50mm (UK 9) hook
IT IS ESSENTIAL TO WORK TO THE STATED TENSION TO ACHIEVE SUCCESS
What you have to do:
Work throughout in openwork pattern. Shape armholes, neck and sleeve tops as indicated. Pick up stitches from neck edges and work collar in main pattern. Work buttonhole band with loops on right front edge.

Instructions

Abbreviations:

beg = beginning

ch = chain

cl = work a cluster as foll: (yrh, insert hook in next st, yrh and draw a loop through, yrh and draw through first 2 loops on hook) over number of sts indicated, yrh and draw through all loops on hook

cm = centimetre(s)

cont = continue

dc = double crochet

foll = follows

patt = pattern

rep = repeat

RS = right side

ss = slip stitch

st(s) = stitch(es)

tr = treble

WS = wrong side

yrh = yarn round hook

BACK:

With 3.50mm (UK 9) hook make 97[107:117]ch.

Foundation row: 1dc in 2nd ch from hook, 1dc in next ch, *miss 3ch, 7tr in next ch, miss 3ch, 1dc in each of next 3ch, rep from * to last 4ch, miss 3ch, 4tr in last ch, turn. 96[106:116] sts. Cont in patt as foll:

1st row: (RS) 1ch (does not count as a st), 1dc in each of first 2 sts, *3ch, 1cl over next 7 sts, 3ch, 1dc in each of next 3 sts, rep from * to last 4 sts, 3ch, 1cl over last 4 sts, turn.

2nd row: 3ch (counts as first tr), 3tr in st at base of ch, *miss 3ch, 1dc in each of next 3dc, miss 3ch, 7tr in next cl, rep from * ending with miss 3ch, 1dc in each of last 2dc, turn.

3rd row: 3ch, miss st at base of ch, 1cl over next 3 sts, *3ch, 1dc in each of next 3 sts, 3ch, 1cl over next 7 sts, rep from * ending with 3ch, 1dc in next st, 1dc in 3rd of 3ch, turn.

4th row: 1ch, 1dc in each of first 2dc, *miss 3ch, 7tr in next cl, miss 3ch, 1dc in each of next 3dc, rep from * ending with miss 3ch, 4tr in 3rd of 3ch, turn.

The last 4 rows form patt. Rep them until Back measures 42[42:40]cm (16½[16½:15¾]in) from beg, ending with a 4th[4th:2nd] row. Fasten off.

Shape armholes:

1st and 2nd sizes only:

Next row: With RS facing, miss first 10 sts and rejoin yarn to centre tr of first 7tr group, 1ch, 1dc in same place as join, 1dc in next tr, *3ch, 1cl over next 7 sts, 3ch, 1dc in each of next 3 sts, rep from * to last 14 sts, 3ch, 1cl over next 4 sts, turn.

3rd size only:

Next row: With RS facing, miss first 10 sts and rejoin yarn to centre dc of first group of 3dc, work as 3rd row to last 12 sts, 3ch, 1dc in each of next 2 sts, turn.

All sizes:

76[86:96] sts. Beg with 2nd[2nd:4th] row, cont in patt on these sts until Back measures 61cm (24in) from beg, ending with a 2nd row. Fasten off.

LEFT FRONT:

With 3.50mm (UK 9) hook make 77[87:97]ch. Work foundation row as given for Back. 76[86:96] sts.

Cont in patt as given for Back until work measures 42[42:40]cm (16½[16½:15¾]in) from beg, ending with a 4th[4th:2nd] row. Fasten off.

Shape armhole:

1st and 2nd sizes only:

Next row: With RS facing, miss first 10 sts and rejoin yarn to centre tr of first 7tr group, 1ch, 1dc in same place as join, 1dc in next tr, patt to end, turn.

3rd size only:

Next row: With RS facing, miss first 10 sts and rejoin yarn to centre dc of first group of 3dc, work as given for 3rd patt row to end, turn.

All sizes:

66[76:86] sts.

Beg with 2nd[2nd:4th] row, cont in patt on these sts until Front measures 53cm (21in) from beg, ending with a 2nd row.

Shape neck and shoulder:

Next row: (RS) Patt 26[36:46] sts, turn and cont on these sts only.

1st size only:

Work straight on these 26 sts until Front measures 61cm (24in) from beg, ending with a 2nd row. Fasten off.

2nd and 3rd sizes only:

Next row: Patt to end, turn.

Next row: (RS) Patt to last 5 sts, turn. [31:41] sts.

Next row: Patt to end.

Next row: Patt to last 5 sts, turn. [26:36] sts.

Work straight on these sts until Front measures 61cm (24in) from beg, ending with a 2nd row. Fasten off.

RIGHT FRONT:

Work as given for Left front, reversing all shapings.

SLEEVES: (make 2

With 3.50mm (UK 9) hook make 77[77:87]ch. Work foundation row as given for Back. 76[76:86] sts. Cont in patt as given for Back until work measures 42[42:44]cm (16½[16½:17¼]in) from beg, ending with a 4th[4th:2nd] row. Fasten off.

Shape sleeve top:

Next row: Work as Back armhole shaping. 56[56:66] sts.

Next row: Patt to last 5 sts, turn.

Rep last row 5[5:7] times more. 26 sts. Fasten off.

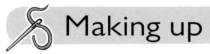 ## Making up

Join shoulder seams.

Collar:

With 3.50mm (UK 9) hook, RS facing and beg at edge of right front neck, work 126[136:136]dc evenly along right front neck, back neck and down left front neck, turn. Cont in patt as given for Back until Collar measures 15[15:16]cm (6[6:6¼in) from beg, ending with a WS row. Fasten off.

Sew in sleeves. Join side and sleeve seams.

Try on cardigan, folding collar down and arranging Right front over Left so that lower edges are aligned. Mark position of snap fastener inside front edges on both pieces and sew in place.

Button loops:

Beg at lower edge of collar point on right front, measure 18cm (7in) down and mark with a pin. With 3.50mm (UK 9) hook and RS facing, work 32dc evenly along right front edge from marked point to collar point, turn and work 1 more row in dc.

Next row: 4ch, miss first st, 1dc in next st, *ss in each of next 8 sts, 1dc in next st, 4ch, 1dc in next st, rep from * twice more. Fasten off. Try on cardigan again and mark positions of buttons on eft front, making sure lower edges are aligned. Sew on buttons.

Chunky bow wrap

Make a pretty present of yourself with this giant bow in a soft, crunchy stitch pattern.

Similar to a large collar, this wrap in a pretty textured pattern sits around the shoulders. It is gathered up at the centre front with a binding strip worked in the same pattern.

GETTING STARTED

 Easy pattern to work and chunky yarn grows quickly.

Size:
Finished wrap measures
105cm (41in) all round x 26cm (10¼in) deep

How much yarn:
4 x 100g (3½oz) balls of Rowan Drift in Samphire (shade 904)

Hook:
10.00mm (UK 000) crochet hook

Tension:
1 patt repeat (6 sts) and 4 rows measure 7.5cm (3in) square over patt on 10.00mm (UK 000) hook
IT IS ESSENTIAL TO WORK TO THE STATED TENSION TO ACHIEVE SUCCESS

What you have to do:
Work wrap in trebles shell pattern separated by double crochet throughout. Join side edges to form wrap. Make narrow binding strip in same pattern and wrap around centre front.

The Yarn
Rowan Drift (approx. 80m/87 yards per 100g/3½oz ball) is 100% merino wool. It is a chunky yarn that is very warm. There is a small range of subtly variegated colours.

Instructions

Abbreviations:

beg = beginning
ch = chain(s)
cm = centimetre(s)
dc = double crochet
foll = following
patt = pattern
rep = repeat
RS = right side
st(s) = stitch(es)
tr = treble

WRAP:

With 10.00mm (UK 000) hook make 88ch for top edge and work downwards.
Foundation row: (RS) Working into back strand only of each ch, 2tr into 4th ch from hook, miss next 2ch, 1dc into foll ch, *miss next 2ch, 5tr (called 1 shell) into foll ch, miss next 2ch, 1dc into foll ch, rep from * to last 3ch, miss next 2ch, 3tr into last ch, turn.

1st patt row: 1ch (counts as first dc), miss st at base of ch and next 2tr, *5tr into next dc, miss next 2tr, 1dc into foll tr (centre tr of shell), rep from * to end, working last dc into 3rd of 3ch, turn.
2nd patt row: 3ch (counts as first tr), 2tr into st at base of ch, miss next 2tr, 1dc into foll tr (centre tr of shell), * 5tr into next dc, miss next 2tr, 1dc into foll tr (centre tr of shell), rep from * ending miss last 2tr, 3tr into 1ch, turn. The last 2 rows form patt. Rep them 5 times more, then work 1st patt row again. Fasten off.

STRIP:

With 10.00mm (UK 000) hook make 10ch.
Foundation row: 2tr into 4th ch from hook, miss next 2ch, 1dc into foll ch, miss next 2ch, 3tr into last ch, turn.
1st patt row: (RS) 1ch (counts as first dc), miss st at base of ch and next 2tr, 5tr into foll dc, miss next 2tr, 1dc into 3rd of 3ch, turn.
2nd patt row: 3ch (counts as first tr), 2tr into st at base of ch, miss next 2tr, 1dc into foll tr (centre tr of shell), miss next 2tr, 3tr into 1ch, turn.
The last 2 rows form patt. Rep them until

work measures approximately 24cm (9½in) from beg. Fasten off.

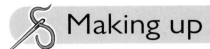 Making up

Join short side edges of wrap together, noting that lower edge has an undulating appearance. Placing seam at centre front of wrap, wind strip around to hide seam and neatly join top and bottom edges. Move seam on strip so that it is hidden on wrong side of wrap and secure with a few stitches.

Cream and pastel throw

Textured granny squares and a soft Aran yarn make this a gorgeous throw for your favourite chair.

The motifs here are based on a variation of the ever-popular granny square. Although retro in feel, the deep pastel shades used in conjunction with the cream border give it a contemporary look.

GETTING STARTED

★★ *Once you have mastered popcorn stitch for square centres, the rest is easy to work but neat assembly is essential.*

Size:
105 x 125cm (41 x 49in)

How much yarn:
15 x 50g (1¾oz) balls of Debbie Bliss Cashmerino Aran in colour A – Cream (shade 101)
3 balls in colour B – Mulberry (shade 042)
2 balls in each of five other colours: C – Deep Lilac (shade 017); D – Pale Blue (shade 202); E – Denim Blue (shade 205); F – Apple Green (shade 502) and G – Soft Pink (shade 603)

Hook:
5.00mm (UK 6) crochet hook

Tension:
Each square measures 20 x 20cm (8 x 8in) on 5.00mm (UK 6) hook
IT IS ESSENTIAL TO WORK TO THE STATED TENSION TO ACHIEVE SUCCESS

What you have to do:
Work individual granny square motifs with popcorn 'flower' at centre. Work one colour at centre with rounds of cream and second colour near outer edge; border each square in cream. Join squares with double crochet seams on RS. Work border with rounds of different basic stitches.

The Yarn
Debbie Bliss Cashmerino Aran (approx. 90m/98 yards per 50g/1¾oz ball) is 55% merino wool, 33% microfibre and 12% cashmere. It produces a soft, machine-washable (at a low temperature) fabric. There is a vast colour range.

Instructions

Abbreviations:

ch = chain
cm = centimetre(s)
dc = double crochet
htr = half treble
rep = repeat(s)
RS = right side
sp(s) = space(s)
ss = slip stitch
st(s) = stitch(es)
tr = treble

MOTIF:

(Make 30 in colours as indicated on diagram.) With 5.00mm (UK 6) hook and first colour (not A), make 7ch, join with a ss into first ch to form a ring.

1st round: 3ch (counts as first tr), 4tr into ring, remove working loop from hook and insert hook in 3rd of 3ch, reinsert hook into working loop and draw through loop on hook — first popcorn st formed, 2ch, *5tr into ring, remove working loop from hook and insert hook in top of first tr, reinsert hook into working loop and draw through loop on hook — 1 popcorn st formed, 2ch, rep from * 6 times more, join with a ss into 3rd of 3ch.

2nd round: Ss into next 2ch sp, 3ch, (2tr, 2ch, 3tr) into same sp — one corner formed, 3tr into next 2ch sp, *(3tr, 2ch, 3tr) into next 2ch sp — corner formed, 3tr into next 2ch sp, rep from * twice more, join with a ss into 3rd of 3ch. Fasten off.

3rd round: Join A to any corner sp, 3ch, (2tr, 2ch, 3tr) into same sp, (miss next 3tr, work 3tr between tr) twice, *(3tr, 2ch, 3tr) into corner sp, (miss next 3tr, work 3tr between tr) twice, rep from * twice more, join with a ss into 3rd of 3ch.

4th round: 3ch, 2tr into sp below ss, *(3tr, 2ch, 3tr) into corner sp, (miss next 3tr, work 3tr between tr) 3 times, rep from * twice more, (3tr, 2ch, 3tr) into corner sp, (miss next 3tr, work 3tr between tr) twice, join with a ss into 3rd of 3ch.

5th round: 3ch, 2tr into sp below ss, miss 3tr, work 3tr between tr, *(3tr, 2ch, 3tr) into corner sp, (miss next 3tr, work 3tr between tr) 4 times, rep from * twice more, (3tr, 2ch, 3tr) into corner sp, (miss next 3tr, work 3tr between tr) twice, join with a ss into 3rd of 3ch. Fasten off.

6th round: Join second colour to any corner sp, 3ch, (2tr, 2ch, 3tr) into corner sp, (miss next 3tr, work 3tr between tr) 5 times, *(3tr, 2ch, 3tr) into corner sp, (miss next 3tr, work 3tr between tr) 5 times, rep from * twice more, join with a ss into 3rd of 3ch.

7th round: 3ch, 1tr into each of next 2tr, *(2tr, 2ch, 2tr) into corner sp, 1tr into each of next 21tr, rep from * twice more, (2tr, 2ch, 2tr) into corner sp, 1tr into each of next 18tr, join with a ss into 3rd of 3ch. Fasten off.

8th round: Join A to any corner sp, 3ch, (1tr, 2ch, 2tr) into corner sp, 1tr into each of next 25tr, *(2tr, 2ch, 2tr) into corner sp, 1tr into each of next 25tr, rep from * twice more, join with a ss into 3rd of 3ch. Fasten off.

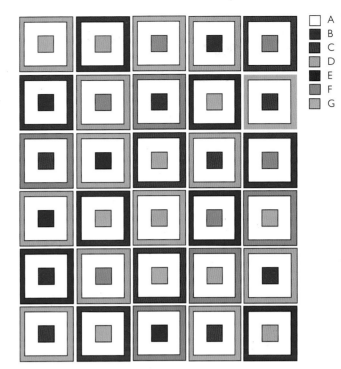

 ## Making up

Arrange motifs in 6 rows containing 5 motifs in each. Either make your own arrangement or use our diagram as a guide. First joining short rows, crochet motifs together on RS of work with A and working in dc. Then crochet rows together in same way to form throw.

Border:

With 5.00mm (UK 6) hook and RS facing, join A onto outer edge of throw, 1ch (counts as first dc), work all around in dc, working 1dc into each tr, 1dc into each join, 1dc into sp at each side of join and 3dc into corner sp, join with a ss into first ch. Fasten off.

Next round: With RS facing, join in B, 2ch (counts as first htr), work all around in htr, working 3htr into centre dc at each corner, join with a ss into 2nd of 2ch. Fasten off.

Next round: With RS facing, join in A, 2ch (counts as first htr), work all around in htr, working 3htr into centre htr at each corner, join with a ss into 2nd of 2ch. Fasten off.

Eco plant pot covers

These covers are a great way to recycle empty tins and hide those unsightly plastic flowerpots.

This eco-conscious project upcycles empty tins with decorative covers, in string, leftover yarn and raffia, for plain plastic flowerpots. Buttons in natural materials are used as trims for the covers.

The Yarn

These projects use a selection of three leftover aran-weight yarns (approx. 75m/82 yards per 50g/1¾oz ball) and three garden strings.

GETTING STARTED

 Very easy fabrics – perfect for a beginner to try to practise working in rounds.

Size:
Large: 13cm (5in) diameter x 16cm (6¼in) high
Medium: 10cm (4in) diameter x 12cm (4¾in) high
Small: 8.5cm (3¼in) diameter x 8.5cm (3¼in) high

How much yarn:
For complete set:
A: 1 x 40m (43 yard) ball of brown jute string
B: 1 x 50g (1¾oz) ball of aran-weight cotton yarn –
we used Debbie Bliss Eco Aran in Pale Blue (shade 616)
C: 1 x 50g (1¾oz) ball of aran-weight wool –
we used Sublime Cashmere Merino Silk Aran in Sage
(shade 08)
D: 1 x 50g (1¾oz) ball of aran-weight denim yarn –
we used Sirdar Denim Aran in Denim Blue (shade 502)
E: 1 x 38m (41 yard) ball of natural cotton twine
F: 1 x 150m (164 yard) reel of green jute string

Hooks:
3.00mm (UK 11) crochet hook
7.00mm (UK 2) crochet hook

Additional items:
3 clean, empty tins in sizes as above
Small and very large tapestry needles
Glue stick, 1 hank of raffia
4 x 2cm (¾in) diameter wooden buttons
15 x 1.5cm (⅝in) diameter coconut shell buttons
2 x small heart-shaped wooden buttons
1 x 3.5cm (1⅜in) vintage button

What you have to do:
Work large and small covers in rounds in stripes of half trebles and variety of string and yarns. Work medium cover in rows in simple textured stitch. Decorate covers with buttons stitched on with raffia. Secure covers to tins at top and bottom edges with a glue stick.

Instructions

Abbreviations:

ch = chain(s)
cm = centimetre(s)
cont = continue
foll = follows
htr = half treble
patt = pattern
rep = repeat
ss = slip stitch
st(s) = stitch(es)
WS = wrong side

Notes:

• Use a safety opener to remove lids from tins and make sure that they have no sharp edges or projecting points around the rim.

• If your tins are printed with designs that show through, you can either paint them to block it out, or cover them with paper before slipping the covers in place.

LARGE COVER:

With 7.00mm (UK 2) hook and A, make 42ch, join with a ss into first ch to form a ring.

1st round: 2ch (counts as first htr), miss st at base of ch, 1htr in each ch to end, join with a ss in 2nd of 2ch. 42 sts.

2nd round: 2ch, miss st at base of ch, working in back loop only work 1htr in each st to end, join with a ss in 2nd of 2ch.

Note: When working into an A round, always work in back loops; when working into rounds in other colours, always work into both loops.

Cont throughout in rounds of htr as set, work in stripe sequence as foll, carrying yarn not in use up WS (inside) of work: 2 rounds each B, C, D, A (fasten off A), B (fasten off B), C (fasten off C) and D (fasten off D).

MEDIUM COVER:

With 7.00mm (UK 2) hook and E, make 25ch.

Foundation row: 1htr into 3rd ch from hook, 1htr into each ch to end, turn. 24 sts.

Patt row: 2ch (counts as first htr), miss st at base of ch, *1htr into front loop only of next st, 1htr into back loop only of next st, rep from * to end, working 1htr in 2nd of 2ch, turn.

Rep patt row 24 times more. Fasten off, leaving a 30cm (12in) tail of twine.

SMALL COVER:

With 7.00mm (UK 2) hook and A, make 28ch, join with a ss into first ch to form a ring.

1st round: 2ch (counts as first htr), miss st at base of ch, 1htr in each ch to end, join with a ss in 2nd of 2ch. 28 sts.

Cont in rounds, carrying yarn not in use up WS (inside) of work.

2nd round: Join in B, 2ch, miss st at base of ch, 1htr in back loop only of each st to end, join with a ss in 2nd of 2ch.
3rd round: Join in F and work as 2nd round but work into both loops of each st.
4th round: With B, work as 2nd round.
5th round: With A, work as 3rd round.
6th round: As 4th round.
7th round: As 3rd round. Fasten off F.
8th round: As 4th round. Fasten off B.
9th round: As 5th round. Fasten off A.

 # Making up

LARGE COVER:
Thread a small tapestry needle with a length of raffia. Pass needle through front of a small button, and then through join of round on 2nd row of 2nd stripe of B. Bring needle back through second hole and tie 2 ends of raffia together with a reef knot. Trim ends so that they are in line with edge of button. Add 11 more buttons in same way, spacing them evenly around cover.
Slip cover over tin and use a glue stick to secure top and bottom edges of cover to top and bottom edges of tin.

MEDIUM COVER:
Thread tail of twine though very large tapestry needle and join top and bottom edges of fabric to form a cylinder. Slip cover over tin and secure top and bottom edges in place with a glue stick.
Tie about 10 strands of raffia round cover, just above centre, and tie in an overhand knot. Trim ends to 3cm (1¼in) and sew the large button over knot using a single length of raffia and small tapestry needle.

SMALL COVER:
Thread small tapestry needle with a length of raffia and sew remaining buttons around tin, spacing them evenly around central A round. Slip cover over tin and secure top and bottom edges in place with a glue stick.

House cushion

Make this house part of your home – and give this cushion pride of place on your favourite chair.

This charming double crochet cushion has a naive house worked within a frame to look like a picture. The details are appliquéd on and embellishments added in embroidery.

GETTING STARTED

 Easy double crochet fabric but working intarsia pattern requires some practice.

Size:
Approximately 45cm (18in) square

How much yarn:
4 x 50g (1¾oz) balls of Rowan Handknit Cotton in colour A – Kingfisher (shade 346)
1 ball in each of four other colours: B – Gooseberry (shade 219); C – Cloud (shade 345); D – Ecru (shade 251) and E – Cassis (shade 351)
Small amount of colour F – Aubergine (shade 348)

Hook:
4.50mm (UK 7) crochet hook

Additional items:
35cm (14in) zip fastener to match colour A
Matching sewing thread and needle
45cm (18in) square cushion pad

Tension:
15 sts and 18 rows measure 10cm (4in) square over dc on 4.50mm (UK 7) hook
IT IS ESSENTIAL TO WORK TO THE STATED TENSION TO ACHIEVE SUCCESS

What you have to do:
Work back of cushion in main colour only and double crochet. Work front of cushion in double crochet and intarsia pattern of grass and sky. Make separate pieces for house, roof, door and door top and sew in place. Embroider details – windows, letterbox and fence – on front. Sew zip fastener into back opening.

The Yarn
Rowan Handknit Cotton (approx. 85m/93 yards per 50g/1¾oz ball) is 100% cotton. It produces a smooth fabric with a matt finish ideal for craft projects as it can be machine washed. There is a good range of colours.

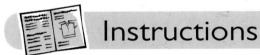 ## Instructions

Note: When working intarsia patt on Front, use a separate ball of A for borders at either side.

BACK:
With 4.50mm (UK 7) hook and A, make 65ch.
Foundation row: (RS) 1dc into 2nd ch from hook, 1dc into each ch to end, turn. 64 sts.
1st row: 1ch (does not count as a st), 1dc into each dc to end, turn.*
Rep last row 72 times more.
74th row: 1ch, 1dc into each of first 8 sts, make 48ch, miss 48 sts, 1dc into each of last 8 sts, turn.
75th row: 1ch, 1dc into each of first 8 sts, 1dc into each of 48ch, 1dc into each of last 8 sts, turn.
76th row: As 1st row. Fasten off.

FRONT:
Work as given for Back to *. Rep last row 8 times more.
10th row: With A, 1ch, 1dc into each of first 8 sts changing to B on last stage of last dc, with B, 1dc into each of next 48 sts changing to A on last stage of last dc, with A, 1dc into each st to end, turn.

Abbreviations:
ch = chain(s)
cm = centimetre(s)
cont = continue
dc = double crochet
dc2tog = (insert hook
in next st, yrh and draw
through a loop) twice, yrh
and draw through all 3
loops on hook
dec = decreased
patt = pattern
rep = repeat
RS = right side
ss = slip stitch
st(s) = stitch(es)
yrh = yarn round hook

Rep last row 23 times more. Cut off B.
34th row: With A, 1ch, 1dc into each of first 8 sts
changing to C on last stage of last dc, with C, 1dc into
each of next 48 sts changing to A on last stage of
last dc, with A, 1dc into each st to end, turn. Rep last
row 33 times more. Cut off C. Cont in A only, work
9 rows more in dc. Fasten off.

HOUSE:
With 4.50mm (UK 7) hook and D, make 29ch. Work
foundation row as given for Back. 28 sts.
Work 26 rows in dc.
27th row: 1ch, dc2tog over first 2 sts, 1dc into each
dc to last 2 sts, dc2tog over last 2 sts, turn. 1 st dec at
each end of row.
28th–33rd rows: As 27th. 14 sts.
34th row: (1st chimney) 1ch, 1dc into each of next 4
sts, turn and work 5 rows on these 4 sts only.
Fasten off.
With RS facing, rejoin D to last 4 sts on last row of
house and work 2nd chimney to match first.

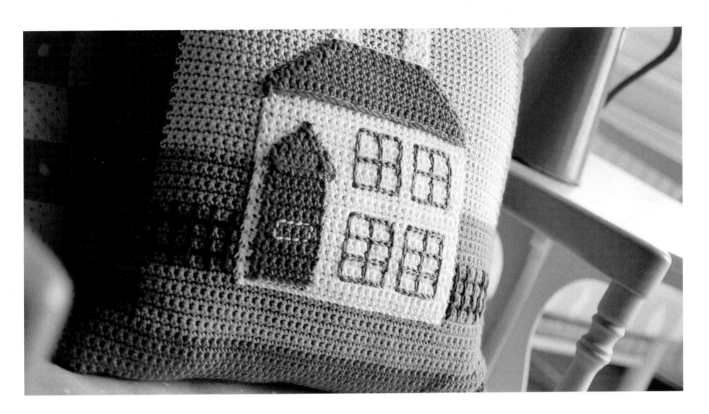

ROOF:

With 4.50mm (UK 7) hook and E, make 29ch.

Foundation row: (RS) Ss into 2nd ch from hook, ss into each ch to end, turn. 28 sts.

1st row: 1ch, miss st at base of ch, 1dc into each st to end, turn.

2nd row: 1ch, dc2tog over first 2 sts, 1dc into each st to last 2 sts, dc2tog over last 2 sts, turn. 1 st dec at each end of row.

3rd–8th rows: As 2nd. 14 sts. Fasten off.

DOOR:

With 4.50mm (UK 7) hook and A, make 8ch. Work foundation row as given for Back. 7 sts.

Work 13 rows in dc. Fasten off.

Top of door:

With 4.50mm (UK 7) hook and E, make 11ch.

Work foundation row as given for Roof. 10 sts.

1st row: 1ch, dc2tog over first 2 sts, 1dc into each st to last 2 sts, dc2tog over last 2 sts, turn. 1 st dec at each end of row.

2nd–4th rows: As 1st. 2 sts.

5th row: 1ch, dc2tog. Fasten off.

Making up

Insert zip behind gap at top of Back; pin, then sew in place with matching thread.

Using photograph as a guide, pin house on Front, then slip stitch neatly in place. Pin roof on top of house and sew in place. Repeat with door and door top. Thread a tapestry needle with a length of A and, beg at bottom right-hand corner of house, count 3 rows up and 2 stitches in from edge and begin stitching window frame in chain stitch, over 6 stitches and 9 rows. Stitch a second window frame between this window frame and door, then stitch two smaller window frames above first 2. With D, stitch a rectangle of backstitch in centre of door for letterbox.

With F, stitch horizontal lines of chain stitch between rows on either side of house, then stitch vertical lines for fence posts.

Scarf with bobble edging

This attractive scarf can be tied or tucked around your neck for a soft draped effect.

Worked in an openwork pattern of shells and chain arches, this triangular scarf is edged in double crochet trimmed with 'popcorn' bobbles.

GETTING STARTED

Once you get the pattern established, it is easy to keep it correct, while shaping at the same time.

Size:
Scarf measures 107cm (42in) across top edge x 44cm (17½in) deep from top edge to point

How much yarn:
2 x 100g (3½oz) balls of King Cole Smooth DK in Grass (shade 887)

Hook:
4.00mm (UK 8) crochet hook

Tension:
24 sts (2 patt reps) measure 9cm (3½in) and 8 rows measure 7cm (2¾in) over patt on 4.00mm (UK 8) hook
IT IS ESSENTIAL TO WORK TO THE STATED TENSION TO ACHIEVE SUCCESS

What you have to do:
Start at lower point of scarf and work throughout in treble shell and chain arch pattern. Increase as directed to form triangular shape of scarf. Work double crochet edging along top edge. Work double crochet and bobble edging along side edges, forming bobbles with popcorn stitches.

The Yarn
King Cole Smooth DK (approx. 216m/235 yards per 100g/3½oz ball) contains 100% microfibre. It produces a soft, easy-care fabric with good stitch definition. The shade range has both pastels and strong modern colours.

Instructions

Abbreviations:

ch = chain(s)

cm = centimetre(s)

cont = continue

dc = double crochet

dtr = double treble

foll = follows

htr = half treble

patt = pattern

popcorn = work 4tr into next dc, drop loop from hook, insert hook from front into top of first of 4tr, pick up dropped loop and draw through loop on hook, work 1ch to secure st

rep(s) = repeat(s)

RS = right side

st(s) = stitch(es)

tr = treble

SCARF:

With 4.00mm (UK 8) hook make 8ch.

1st row: (RS) 1dc into 2nd ch from hook, miss 2ch, 5tr into next ch, miss 2ch, 1dc into last ch, turn. 1 × 5tr shell.

2nd row: 1ch (does not count as a st), 1dc into st at base of ch, 5ch, 1dc into 3rd of next 5tr shell, 5ch, 1dc into last dc, turn. 2 × 5ch arches.

3rd row: 4ch (counts as first dtr), 5tr into st at base of 4ch, 1dc into next 5ch arch, 5ch, 1dc into next 5ch arch, 5tr into last dc, 1dtr into same place as 5tr, turn. 2 × 5tr shells.

4th row: 1ch, 1dc into st at base of ch, 5ch, 1dc into 3rd of next 5tr shell, 5ch, 1dc into next 5ch arch, 5ch, 1dc into 3rd of next 5tr shell, 5ch, 1dc into top of turning ch, turn. 4 × 5ch arches.

5th row: 4ch, 5tr into st at base of 4ch, (1dc into next 5ch arch, 5ch, 1dc into next 5ch arch, 5tr into next dc) twice, 1dtr in same place as last 5tr, turn. 3 x 5tr shells.

6th row: 1ch, 1dc into st at base of ch, (5ch, 1dc into 3rd of next 5tr shell, 5ch, 1dc into next 5ch arch) twice, 5ch, 1dc into 3rd of next 5tr shell, 5ch, 1dc into top of turning ch, turn. 6 x 5ch arches.

7th row: 4ch, 5tr into st at base of 4ch, (1dc into next 5ch arch, 5ch, 1dc into next 5ch arch, 5tr into next dc) 3 times, 1dtr into same place as 5tr, turn. 4 x 5tr shells.

8th row: 1ch, 1dc into st at base of ch, (5ch, 1dc into 3rd of next 5tr shell, 5ch, 1dc into next 5ch arch) 3 times, 5ch, 1dc into 3rd of next 5tr shell, 5ch, 1dc into top of turning ch, turn. 8 x 5ch arches.

9th row: 4ch, 5tr into st at base of 4ch, (1dc into next 5ch arch, 5ch, 1dc into next 5ch arch, 5tr into next dc) 4 times, 1dtr into same place as last 5tr, turn. 5 x 5tr shells.

10th row: 1ch, 1dc into st at base of ch, (5ch, 1dc into 3rd of next 5tr shell, 5ch, 1dc into next 5ch arch) 4 times, 5ch, 1dc into 3rd of next 5tr shell, 5ch, 1dc into top of turning ch, turn. 10 x 5ch arches.

Cont as now set for a further 34 rows, increasing by working one more rep of patt (instructions in brackets) on every 2 rows. (44 x 5ch arches.)
Fasten off.

Top edging:
With 4.00mm (UK 8) hook and RS of work facing, rejoin yarn to right-hand corner of straight top edge and cont as foll:

Next row: 1ch (does not count as a st), 1dc into st at base of ch, (3dc into next 5ch arch, 1dc into next dc) to end, turn. 177 sts.

Next row: 1ch, 1dc into st at base of ch, 1dc in each dc to end, turn.
Work 1 row more in dc. Fasten off.

Bobble edging:
With 4.00mm (UK 8) hook and RS of work facing, rejoin yarn to end of border at top edge and work down shaped sides as foll:

1st row: 1ch (does not count as a st), work 2dc into row-ends of top edging, work 88dc along first shaped edge (working 1dc into dc at end of every arch row and 3dc into dtr at end of every 5tr shell row), work 88dc along second shaped edge and 2dc into row-ends of top edging. 180dc.
Work 2 rows in dc.

4th row: 4ch (counts as 1htr, 2ch), miss first 2dc, 1dc into next dc, (5ch, miss 4dc, 1dc into next dc) to last 2dc, 2ch, miss 1dc, 1htr into last dc, turn.

5th row: 1ch, 1dc into st at base of ch, 3ch, 1 popcorn into first dc, (3ch, 1dc into next 5ch arch, 3ch, 1 popcorn into next dc) to end, ending 3ch, 1dc into 2nd of 4ch. Fasten off.

Sweater with patterned sleeves

Wear the pattern on your sleeve with this distinctive sweater.

Contrasting plain body with openwork patterned sleeves and ribbed edgings, this raglan sweater is a contemporary version of a classic favourite.

GETTING STARTED

★★ *This garment is not as complicated as it looks, although there is a lot of shaping for raglan armholes.*

Size:
To fit bust: 81[86:91:96]cm (32[34:36:38]in)
Actual size: 90[95:100.5:106]cm
(35½[37½:39½:41¾]in)
Length: 59.5[62:62:64]cm (23½[24½:24½:25½]in)
Sleeve seam: 48cm (19in)
Note: Figures in square brackets [ ] refer to larger sizes; where there is only one set of figures, it applies to all sizes

How much yarn:
11[12:13:14] x 50g (1¾oz) balls of Debbie Bliss Amalfi in Pale Turquoise (shade 23)

Hook:
4.00mm (UK 8) crochet hook

Tension:
15.5 sts and 8.5 rows measure 10cm (4in) square over tr on 4.00mm (UK 8) hook
IT IS ESSENTIAL TO WORK TO THE STATED TENSION TO ACHIEVE SUCCESS

What you have to do:
Work hem, cuff and neckband in relief trebles for mock rib. Work front and back in trebles, shaping raglan armholes and neck as directed in instructions. Work sleeves in openwork pattern separated by rows of trebles, shaping raglan sleeve tops as directed.

The Yarn
Debbie Bliss Amalfi (approx. 100m/109 yards per 50g/1¾oz ball) contains 70% cotton, 15% viscose, 10% linen and 5% silk. It produces a soft luxurious fabric with an interesting sheen and texture, and it should be hand washed only. There are many delicious summer shades.

 Instructions

BACK:
With 4.00mm (UK 8) hook make 72[76:80:84]ch.
Foundation row: (RS) 1tr into 4th ch from hook, 1tr into each ch to end, turn. 70[74:78:82] sts.
Rib row: 3ch (counts as first tr), miss st at base of ch, *1trb around next st, 1trf around next st, rep from * to end, 1tr into 3rd of 3ch, turn.
Rep rib row 4 times more.
Next row: (RS) 3ch, miss st at base of ch, 1tr into each tr to end, working last tr into 3rd of 3ch, turn.
Rep last row until work measures 30cm (12in) from beg, ending with a WS row.
Shape raglan armholes:
Next row: Ss into each of first 5tr, 3ch, miss st at base of ch, 1tr into each tr to last 4 sts, turn. 62[66:70:74] sts.
Next row: 3ch, miss st at base of ch and next tr, 1tr into each tr to last 2 sts, miss next tr, 1tr into 3rd of 3ch, turn. 1 st dec at each end of row.**
Rep last row until 24[24:28:28] sts rem. Fasten off.

Abbreviations:

beg = beginning
ch = chain(s)
cm = centimetre(s)
cont = continue
dc = double crochet
dec = decrease(d)
foll = follows
inc = increase(d)
patt = pattern
rem = remain(ing)
rep = repeat
RS = right side
rtrb = relief tr back: work tr in usual way but around stem of next st, inserting hook from right to left and back to front
rtrf = relief tr front: work tr in usual way but around stem of next st, inserting hook from right to left and front to back
sp = space
ss = slip stitch
st(s) = stitch(es)
tr = treble
tr2tog = (yrh, insert hook in next st, yrh and draw through a loop, yrh and draw through first two loops on hook) twice, yrh and draw through all 3 loops on hook
WS = wrong side
yrh = yarn round hook

FRONT:
Work as given for Back to **.
Rep last row until 28[28:32:32] sts rem, ending with a WS row.

Shape neck:
Next row: (RS) 3ch, miss st at base of ch and next st, 1tr into each of next 3tr, tr2tog over next 2 sts, turn and complete this side of neck first. 5 sts.

Next row: 3ch, miss st at base of ch, tr2tog over next 2 sts, miss last tr, 1tr into

3rd of 3ch. 3 sts. Fasten off.
With RS of work facing, miss centre 14[14:18:18] sts, rejoin yarn in next st, 3ch, miss st at base of ch, tr2tog over next 2 sts, 1tr into each of next 2tr, miss next tr, 1tr into 3rd of 3ch, turn. 5 sts.

Next row: 3ch, miss st at base of ch and next tr, 1tr in next tr, tr2tog over next 2 sts. 3 sts. Fasten off.

SLEEVES: (make 2)
With 4.00mm (UK 8) hook make 38[42:42:46]ch. Work foundation row as given for Back. 36[40:40:44] sts. Work 6 rows in rib as given for Back, ending with a RS row.

Inc row: (WS) 3ch, miss st at base of ch, patt 2[4:4:3] sts, (work twice into next st, patt 4[4:4:5] sts) 6 times, work twice into next st, patt to end, turn. 43[47:47:51] sts.
Cont in patt as foll:

1st row: (RS) 3ch (counts as first tr), miss st at base of ch, 1tr into each st to end, working last tr in 3rd of 3ch, turn.

2nd row: 4ch (counts as 1tr, 1ch), *miss next 3tr, (1tr, 1ch, 1tr) into next tr, 1ch, rep from * to last 3 sts, miss next 2tr, 1tr into 3rd of 3ch, turn.

3rd row: 3ch, miss st at base of ch, *1tr in next 1ch sp, 1tr in next tr, rep from * ending 1tr in 4th of 4ch and 1tr in 3rd of 4ch, turn.

4th row: 4ch, miss st at base of ch, 1tr

into next tr, *1ch, miss 3tr, (1tr, 1ch, 1tr) into next tr, rep from * to last 5 sts, 1ch, miss next 3tr, 1tr into next tr, 1ch, 1tr into 3rd of 3ch, turn.

5th row: As 3rd row.

2nd to 5th rows set patt.

6th row: As 2nd row.

7th row: 3ch, 1tr in first tr, *1tr into next 1ch sp, 1tr into next tr, rep from * ending 1tr into 4th of 4ch, 2tr into 3rd of 4ch, turn. 1 st inc at each end.

8th row: 3ch, 1tr into first tr, miss next tr, *(1tr, 1ch, 1tr) into next tr, 1ch, miss next 3tr, rep from * to last 3 sts, 1tr into next tr, 1ch, 1tr into next tr, 2tr into 3rd of 3ch, turn. 1 st inc at each end.

9th row: 3ch, 1tr into first tr, 1tr into each of next 2tr, *1tr into 1ch sp, 1tr into next tr, rep from * to last 2 sts, 1tr into next tr, 2tr into 3rd of 3ch, turn. 1 st inc at each end.

10th row: 4ch, miss first 2tr, *(1tr, 1ch, 1tr) into next tr, 1ch, miss next 3tr, rep from * to last 3 sts, (1tr, 1ch, 1tr) into next tr, 1ch, miss 1tr, 1tr into 3rd of 3ch, turn. 1 st inc at each end. 51[55:55:59] sts.

Rep 3rd to 10th rows once, then work 3rd to 8th rows again. 63[67:67:71] sts.

Next row: 3ch, miss st at base of ch, 1tr into next tr, *1tr into next tr, 1tr into next ch, rep from * to last 3 sts, 1tr into each of next 2tr, 1tr into 3rd of 3ch, turn.

Work 4th and 5th rows, then work 2nd to 5th rows.

Shape raglan sleeve top:

Next row: (WS) Ss into each of first 5 sts, 4ch (counts as 1tr, 1ch), miss next 2 sts, *(1tr, 1ch, 1tr) into next tr, 1ch, miss next 3tr, rep from * to last 8 sts, (1tr, 1ch, 1tr) into next tr, 1ch, miss next 2tr, 1tr into next tr, turn. 55[59:59:63] sts.

1st dec row: 3ch, miss st at base of ch, miss next 1ch sp and 1tr, 1tr into next 1ch sp, *1tr into next tr, 1tr into next 1ch sp, rep from * to last 3 sts, miss next tr and 1ch sp, 1tr into 3rd of 3ch, turn. 2 sts dec at each end.

2nd dec row: 4ch, *miss next 3tr, (1tr, 1ch, 1tr) into next tr, 1ch, rep from * to last 3 sts, miss next 2 sts, 1tr into 3rd of 3ch.

Rep last 2 rows 8[9:9:10] times more. 19 sts.

Next row: 3ch, 1tr into each 1ch sp and tr, ending 1tr into 4th of 4ch and 1tr into 3rd of 4ch. 19 sts. Fasten off.

NECKBAND:

Join raglan seams.

With 4.00mm (UK 8) hook and RS of work facing, join yarn to left back raglan seam, 1ch, work 1dc into each st on left sleeve top, 6dc evenly down left front neck, 1dc into each st along centre front neck, 6dc evenly up right front neck, 1dc into each st on right sleeve top and 1dc into each st across back neck, join with a ss into first dc. 88[88:96:96] sts.

1st round: 3ch (counts as first tr), miss st at base of ch, 1tr into each st, join with a ss into 3rd of 3ch.

2nd round: 3ch, miss st at base of ch, *1rtrf around next st, 1rtrb around next st, rep from * ending 1rtrf around last st, join with a ss into 3rd of 3ch.

Rep last round twice more. Fasten off.

Making up

Join side and sleeve seams.

Velvet-trimmed scarf

Velvet ribbon and beads make great decorations
for this textured scarf.

This pretty shell-patterned scarf is given a luxurious touch with sewn-on velvet ribbons and a shop-bought beaded fringe.

The Yarn
Sirdar Snuggly Baby Bamboo DK (approx. 95m/104 yards per 50g/1¾oz ball) contains 80% bamboo-sourced viscose and 20% wool. It produces a soft fabric with a subtle sheen that should be hand-washed once it has the trimmings added. Available colours include a mix of both pastel shades and plenty of brights.

GETTING STARTED

 Shell pattern is easy to work once you get going but care is needed with sewing on the trimmings.

Size:
Finished scarf is 20 x 140cm (8 x 55in), excluding fringe

How much yarn:
5 x 50g (1¾oz) balls of Sirdar Snuggly Baby Bamboo DK in Putty (shade 132)

Hook:
4.00mm (UK 8) crochet hook

Additional items:
55cm (22in) of beaded fringe or trim
1.8m (2 yards) of 15mm- (⅝in)wide single face velvet ribbon in apple green

90cm (1 yard) of 10mm- (⅜ in-) wide single face velvet ribbon in old gold
90cm (1 yard) of 20mm- (¾in-) wide single face velvet ribbon in mid brown
Matching sewing threads and needle

Tension:
4 shells measure 9cm (3½in) across and 10 rows measure 10cm (4in) deep over patt on 4.00mm (UK 8) crochet hook
IT IS ESSENTIAL TO WORK TO THE STATED TENSION TO ACHIEVE SUCCESS

What you have to do:
Work a foundation row of treble shells. Continue throughout in an interlocking shell pattern. Sew beaded trim to ends of scarf. Trim each end of scarf with sewn-on bands of velvet ribbon in different colours.

Instructions

Abbreviations:

beg = beginning
ch = chain
cm = centimetre(s)
dc = double crochet
patt = pattern
rep = repeat
RS = right side
sp = space
ss = slip stitch
tr = treble
tr2tog = (yrh, insert hook into next st and draw a loop through, yrh and draw through first two loops on hook) twice, yrh and draw through all 3 loops on hook
WS = wrong side
yrh = yarn round hook

SCARF:
With 4.00mm (UK 8) hook make 40ch loosely.
Foundation row: (RS) 4tr into 4th ch from hook, * miss next 3ch, ss into next ch, 3ch (counts as 1tr), 4tr into same ch as ss – called 1 shell, rep from * 7 times more, missnext 3 ch ss into last ch, turn.
1st row: 3ch, *tr2tog over 2nd and 3rd tr of next shell, 3ch, 1dc into sp between last tr of shell and 3ch, rep from * 8 times more, turn.

2nd row: 3ch, 4tr into first dc, *ss into next dc, 3ch, 4tr into same dc as ss, rep from * 7 times more, ss into sp between final st and 3ch, turn.

The last 2 rows form patt. Rep them until scarf measures 140cm (55in) from beg, ending with a 1st row. Fasten off.

 ## Making up

Cut beaded fringe into two x 22cm (8½in) lengths, ensuring that beads are centred and there is an equal amount of spare tape at each end. Tack under a 1cm (½in) turning at ends and pin tape heading to scarf so that beads hang below the foundation and finishing rows. Sew in place.

Cut ribbon into lengths twice the width of the scarf plus 2cm (¾in). Press under a 1cm (½in) turning at each end. Fold a length of green ribbon around one end of scarf and pin in place so that one side conceals tape heading of fringe. Slip stitch folded ends together and sew top and bottom edges of ribbon to scarf.

Add a gold, brown and another green ribbon (as shown in photograph), making sure they are all parallel. Trim the other end of the scarf in the same way.

Bow-trimmed bag

Crochet this delightful mesh bag and decorate it with
a charming little bow.

Worked in a chain mesh pattern and lined with fabric, this pretty little bag has drawstring cords and bow trim worked in a toning colour.

GETTING STARTED

⭐⭐ *Straight piece of fabric assembly but take care with working chain mesh and making up bag.*

Size:
Bag measures approximately 24cm (9½in) wide x 29cm (11½in) high

How much yarn:
2 x 50g (1¾oz) balls of DMC Natura Just Cotton in colour A – Bourgogne (shade N34)
1 ball in colour B – Amaranto (shade N33)

Hook:
3.00mm (UK 11) crochet hook

Additional items:
51 x 28cm (20 x 11in) piece of lining fabric
Matching thread and sewing needle
3 small buttons

Tension:
6 ch sps and 14 rows measure 10cm (4in) square over patt on 3.00mm (UK 11) hook
IT IS ESSENTIAL TO WORK TO THE STATED TENSION TO ACHIEVE SUCCESS

What you have to do:
Work bag in one piece in chain mesh pattern, incorporating double crochet channels for drawsting. Make cords in slip stitch and bow in double crochet. Sew simple fabric lining for bag.

The Yarn
DMC Natura Just Cotton (approx. 155m/ 169 yards per 50g/1¾oz ball) contains 100% combed cotton threads and has a matt finish. Ideal for crafts, it has 34 vibrant shades.

Instructions

BAG:

With 3.00mm (UK 11) hook and A,
make 122ch.

Foundation row: (RS) 1dc into 10th ch from hook, *
5ch, miss 3ch, 1dc into next ch, rep from * to end, turn. 29
sps/29dc.

Patt row: 5ch, 1dc into first 5ch sp, * 5ch, 1dc into next
sp, rep from * to end, turn.

Rep last row until work, when slightly stretched, measures
23cm (9in) from beg, ending with a WS row.

Make drawstring channel:

Next row: 1ch (does not count as a st), 1dc into first dc,
* miss 1ch, 1dc into each of next 3ch, miss 1ch, 1dc into
next dc, rep from * to last sp, 1dc into each of next 2ch,
turn. 115 sts.

Next row: 1ch, 1dc into first dc, * 2ch, miss 2dc in row
below, 1dc into each of next 51dc, 2ch, miss 2dc in row
below*, 1dc into each of next 2dc, rep from * to * once
more, 1dc into each of last 2 sts, turn.

Next row: 1ch, 1dc into first dc, 1dc into each dc and 1dc
into each ch to end, turn. 115dc.

Next row: 5ch, miss first 2dc, 1dc into next dc, * 5ch, miss
3dc, 1dc into next dc, rep from * to end, turn. 29 sps.

Rep patt row until work, when slightly stretched, measures
29cm (11½in) from beg, ending with a WS row. Fasten off.

CORDS: (make 2)

With 3.00mm (UK 11) hook and B, make 158ch.

Next row: Ss into 2nd ch from hook, ss into each ch to
end. Fasten off.

Cord ends: (make 2)

With 3.00mm (UK 11) hook and B, make 5ch.

Foundation row: 1dc into 2nd ch from hook, 1dc into
each ch to end, turn. 4dc. Work 5 rows in dc. Fasten off.

BOW:

With 3.00mm (UK 11) hook and B, make 10ch.

Foundation row: 1dc into 2nd ch from hook, 1dc into

each ch to end, turn. 9dc.

Work 31 rows in dc. Fasten off.

Tails: (make 2)

With 3.00mm (UK 11) hook and B, make 6ch. Work foundation row (5dc) and 11 rows in dc as given for Bow. Fasten off.

Middle strip:

With 3.00mm (UK 11) hook and B, make 4ch. Work foundation row (3dc) and 11 rows in dc as given for Bow. Fasten off.

 ## Making up

Fold crochet mesh piece in half, with RS facing, and sew side and bottom seams. Turn RS side out.

Sew short ends of bow together and flatten it with seam at centre back. Wrap middle strip around centre and pull tight to form a bow; sew in place. Fold each tail in half lengthways and sew behind bow. Sew complete bow to centre front of bag at dc channel section, then sew a button to middle of bow.

Fold lining fabric in half and sew bottom and side edges, taking a 1.5cm (⅝in) seam allowance. Turn under top edge by 1.5cm (⅝in), press and sew. Place lining inside crochet bag (top of lining should be level with top of dc channel rows) and pin in place. Sew through crochet bag and lining either side of dc rows to form a channel for drawstrings. Next, attach a safety-pin to one end of one cord and thread this through a ch sp in dc rows at side seam of bag, then through channel and back out of hole adjacent to first hole. Repeat with other cord at opposite side of bag. Fold each cord end piece over both ends of cord and sew to secure. Sew a button on each one.

Motif peg bag

This retro-style peg bag makes a useful and attractive addition to your washing line.

The front of this colourful peg bag consists of small patchwork motifs with a 'floral' centre, while the back is worked in rounds of trebles. You can see the vibrant fabric lining through the slot opening on the front.

The Yarn

Sirdar Snuggly Baby Bamboo DK (approx. 95m/104 yards per 50g/1¾oz ball) contains 80% bamboo-sourced viscose and 20% wool. Machine-washable, it is practical and hard-wearing and there is a good range of shades suitable for lively colour work.

GETTING STARTED

 Joining motifs as you work sounds complicated but becomes easier once you have practised a few.

Size:

Bag measures approximately 28 x 30cm (11 x 12in)

How much yarn:

2 x 50g (1¾oz) balls of Sirdar Snuggly Baby Bamboo DK in each of three colours: A – Paintbox Pink (shade 160); B – Jack in a Box (shade 159); C – Yummy Yellow (shade 123)

Hook:

4.00mm (UK 8) crochet hook

Additional items:

30 x 64cm (12 x 25in) rectangle of pink cotton fabric
Sewing threads in pink and turquoise
Straight wooden clothes hanger 26cm (10in) long

Tension:

One motif measures 4cm (1½in) square; first 3 rounds of back measure 7cm (2¾in) square worked on 4.00mm (UK 8) hook
IT IS ESSENTIAL TO WORK TO THE STATED TENSION TO ACHIEVE SUCCESS

What you have to do:

Work front in rows of square motifs, joining each to the previous one as you work. Each motif is worked in two colours and colours are alternated throughout. Work back as one large granny square, alternating three colours throughout. Sew fabric lining for bag.

Instructions

Abbreviations:

ch = chain(s)

cm = centimetre(s)

cont = continue

dc = double crochet

rep = repeat

RS = right side

sp = space

ss = slip stitch

tr = treble

WS = wrong side

Note: Square motifs are joined together in horizontal rows from left to right as you work, beginning at top left corner.

FRONT:
1st row:

1st motif: With 4.00mm (UK 8) hook and A, make 5ch, join with a ss into first ch to form a ring.

1st round: 3ch, work 4tr into ring, remove hook from working loop and insert it into 3rd of 3ch, put working loop back on hook and draw through loop already on hook, 2ch, (work 5tr into ring, remove hook from working loop and insert it into top of first of 5tr, replace working loop on hook and draw through loop already on hook – 1 popcorn st completed, 2ch) 3 times, join with a ss into 3rd of 3ch. Fasten off.

2nd round: Join B to any 2ch sp, (3ch, 2tr, 2ch, 3tr) into same sp, (3tr, 2ch, 3tr into next ch sp) 3 times, join with a ss into 3rd of 3ch. Fasten off.

2nd motif: With B, work as given for 1st

motif to completion of 1st round.

2nd (joining) round: Join C to any 2ch sp, (3ch, 2tr, 2ch, 3tr) into same sp, (3tr, 2ch, 3tr) into next 2ch sp, 3tr into next 2ch sp, ss into 2ch sp of 1st motif, 3tr into same ch sp on 2nd motif, 3tr into next 2ch sp on 2nd motif, ss into next 2ch sp of 1st motif, 3tr into same ch sp on 2nd motif, join with a ss into 3rd of 3ch. Fasten off.

3rd motif: Work as given for 2nd motif, using C for 1st round and A for 2nd round.

Complete 1st row by working 4 more motifs, repeating colour sequence given, then working another motif in same colours as 1st motif. Join each motif to previous one on 2nd round as given for 2nd motif.

2nd row:

1st motif: Work 1st round in B and 2nd round in C, joining to 1st motif of 1st row.

2nd motif: Work 1st round in C.

2nd (joining) round: Join A to any 2ch sp, (3ch, 2tr, 2ch, 3tr) into same sp, 3tr into next 2ch sp, ss into bottom right-hand sp of 2nd motif on 1st row, 3tr into same ch sp on 2nd motif, 3tr into next 2ch sp, ss into bottom right-hand sp of 1st motif on

1st row, 3tr into same ch sp on 2nd motif, 3tr into next ch sp, ss into bottom right-hand sp of 1st motif on 2nd row, 3tr into same sp on 2nd motif, join with a ss into 3rd of 3ch. Fasten off.

3rd motif: Work as given for 2nd motif, working 1st round in A and 2nd round in B.

Complete 2nd row by working 4 more motifs, repeating colour sequence of 2nd row and then working another motif in same colours as 1st motif.

3rd row:

1st motif: Work 1st round in C and 2nd round in A.

2nd motif: Work 1st round in A and 2nd round in B. Now miss next 3 motifs in 2nd row and cont as foll:

3rd motif: Work 1st round in B and 2nd round in C.

4th motif: Work 1st round in C and 2nd round in A.

4th row:

Work 7 motifs in same colours as 1st row, working across gap left in previous row to create rectangular opening.

5th row: Work motifs in colours as 2nd row.

6th row: Work 1st and 2nd motifs in colours as 3rd row. Work 3rd motif using B for 1st round and C for 2nd round. Complete 6th row by working 4 more motifs, repeating colour sequence given, then working another motif in same colours as 1st motif.

7th and 8th rows: Work motifs in colours as 1st and 2nd rows.

Opening edging:

With 4.00mm (UK 8) hook and B, work neatly in dc around rectangular opening. Fasten off.

BACK:

With 4.00mm (UK 8) hook and B, make 5ch, join with a ss into first ch to form a ring.

1st round: 3ch, 2tr into ring, (2ch, 3tr into ring) 3 times, 2ch, join with a ss into 3rd of 3ch. Fasten off.

2nd round: Join A to any 2ch (corner) sp, 3ch, 2tr, 2ch, 3tr into same sp, (3tr, 2ch, 3tr into next corner sp) 3 times, join with a ss into 3rd of 3ch. Fasten off.

3rd round: Join C to any 2ch (corner) sp, 3ch, 2tr, 2ch, 3tr into same sp, *3tr into next sp between groups of tr, (3tr, 2ch, 3tr) into next corner sp, rep from * twice more, 3tr into next sp between groups of tr, join with a ss into 3rd of 3ch. Fasten off.

Work 11 more rounds in colour sequence as set, adding one more group of 3tr to each side of each round. Fasten off.

Making up

With WS facing, pin one edge of Back to top edge of Front. With A, oversew adjacent edges. Pin two bottom edges together, then pin side edges together from bottom corners upwards, allowing top row of motifs to fold in half onto Back. Join with a row of dc worked with B.

Lining:

Fold cotton fabric in half to form a square. Sew three raw edges together, taking a 1cm (⅜in) seam allowance. Clip corners and trim seam allowance to 5mm (¼in). Mark an 8cm (3in) line in the centre of one side, 8cm (3in) below folded edge. Carefully snip along this line and turn lining RS out through opening. Ease out corners and press. Cut a small notch in centre of folded edge for hook of hanger.

Push lining into bag so that slit lines up with centre of opening. Cut outwards from each corner and fold resulting flaps forwards so that they lie under bag front. Pin bag front to lining around opening and oversew with turquoise sewing thread.

Insert hanger through opening and feed hook through notch in top edge of lining and then through foundation ring in centre of middle square in top row.

Chunky cowl-neck sweater

This over-sized sweater will see you through the winter chill in style.

Over-sized with a floppy cowl collar, this chunky sweater, worked in amazing space-dyed yarn and a chevron stitch pattern, has a casual, laid-back appearance.

The Yarn

Sirdar Indie (approx. 43m/47 yards per 50g/1¾oz ball) contains 51% wool and 49% acrylic. It is a light yet chunky, machine-washable yarn, available in a wide range of exciting variegated colours.

GETTING STARTED

 Simple pattern but working chevron pattern requires concentration.

Size:
To fit bust: 81–86[91–97]cm (32–34[36–38]in)
Actual size: 112[134]cm (44[53]in)
Length: 67cm (26½in)
Sleeve seam: 45cm (17¾in)
Note: Figures in square brackets [ ] refer to larger size; where there is only one set of figures, it applies to both sizes

How much yarn:
22[24] x 50g (1¾oz) balls of Sirdar Indie in Variegated Blue (shade 166)

Hook:
8.00mm (UK 0) crochet hook

Tension:
10 sts (1 patt rep) measures 11cm (4¼in) and 4 rows measure 9cm (3½in) over patt on 8.00mm (UK 0) hook
IT IS ESSENTIAL TO WORK TO THE STATED TENSION TO ACHIEVE SUCCESS

What you have to do:
Work throughout in chevron pattern. Shape front neck and sleeves as indicated. Work cowl collar directly onto neckline, working in rounds and shaping as indicated.

Instructions

Abbreviations:

beg = beginning
ch = chain
cm = centimetre(s)
inc = increase(d)
patt = pattern
rep = repeat
RS = right side
ss = slip stitch
st(s) = stitch(es)
tog = together
tr = treble
tr3tog = work 1tr into
each of next 3 sts as
indicated leaving last
loop of each on hook,
yrh and draw through
all 4 loops
WS = wrong side
yrh = yarn round hook

BACK:

With 8.00mm (UK 0) hook make 54[64]ch.
Foundation row: (RS) 1tr into 4th ch from hook, *1tr into each of next 3ch, tr3tog over next 3ch, 1tr into each of next 3ch, 3tr into next ch, rep from * to end, working 2tr (instead of 3tr) into last ch, turn. 51[61] sts.

1st row: 3ch (counts as first tr), 1tr into st at base of ch, *1tr into each of next 3tr, tr3tog over next 3tr, 1tr into each of next 3tr, 3tr into next tr, rep from * to end, working 2tr (instead of 3tr) into 3rd of 3ch, turn. Rep last row until work measures 60cm (23½in) from beg, ending with a RS row.**

Next row: 3ch, miss st at base of ch, 1tr into each st to end, working last tr into 3rd of 3ch, turn. 51[61] sts.
Rep last row twice more. Fasten off.

FRONT:

Work as given for Back to **.
Shape neck:
Next row: (WS) 3ch, miss st at base of ch, 1tr into each of next 19[24] sts, turn and complete this side of neck first.
Next row: Ss into each of first 4 sts, 3ch, miss st at base of ch, 1tr into each tr to end, working last tr into 3rd of 3ch, turn.
Next row: 3ch, miss st at base of ch, 1tr

into each of next 14[19]tr. Fasten off. With WS of work facing, miss centre 11 sts at base of neck and rejoin yarn to next st.

Next row: 3ch, miss st at base of ch, 1tr into each st to end, working last tr into 3rd of 3ch, turn.

Next row: 3ch, miss st at base of ch, 1tr into each of next 16[21]tr, turn.

Next row: Ss into each of first 3 sts, 3ch, miss st at base of ch, 1tr into each tr to end, working last tr into 3rd of 3ch. Fasten off.

SLEEVES: (make 2

With 8.00mm (UK 0) hook make 36ch.

Foundation row: (RS) 1tr into 4th ch from hook, *1tr into each of next 2ch, tr3tog over next 3ch, 1tr into each of next 2ch, 3tr into next ch, rep from * to end, working 2tr (instead of 3tr) into last ch, turn. 33 sts.

1st row: 3ch (counts as first tr), 1tr into st at base of ch, *1tr into each of next 2tr, tr3tog over next 3tr, 1tr into each of next 2tr, 3tr into next tr, rep from * to end, working 2tr (instead of 3tr) into 3rd of 3ch, turn. Rep last row 3 times more.

Inc row: (WS) 3ch, 1tr into st at base of ch, *1tr into next tr, 2tr into next tr, tr3tog over next 3tr, 2tr into next tr, 1tr into next tr, 3tr into next tr, rep from * to end, working 2tr (instead of 3tr) into 3rd of 3ch, turn. 8 sts inc.

Next row: 3ch (counts as first tr), 1tr into st at base of ch, *1tr into each of next 3tr, tr3tog over next 3tr, 1tr into each of next 3tr, 3tr into next tr, rep from * to end, working 2tr (instead of 3tr) into 3rd of 3ch, turn. 41 sts.

Rep last row until work measures approximately 43cm (17in) from beg, ending with a RS row.

Next row: 3ch, miss st at base of ch, 1tr into each st to end, working last tr into 3rd of 3ch. Fasten off.

COWL NECK:

Join shoulder seams.

With 8.00mm (UK 0) hook and RS of work facing, join yarn to neck edge at left shoulder seam, 3ch (counts as first tr), work 11tr evenly down left front neck, 1tr into each of 11tr at centre front neck, work 11tr evenly up right front neck and 1tr into each of 21tr across back neck, join with a ss into 3rd of 3ch. 55 sts.

1st round: 3ch, miss st at base of ch, 1tr into each tr to end, join with a ss into 3rd of 3ch.

Rep last round 3 times more, turning at end of last round so inside of cowl neck is facing.

Work 4 more rounds, turning at end of each round.

Inc round: 3ch, miss st at base of ch, *1tr into each of next 4tr, 2tr into next tr, rep from * to last 4 sts, 1tr into each of last 4tr, 1tr into base of 3ch, join with a ss into 3rd of 3ch, turn. 66 sts.

Work 2 more rounds in tr, turning at end of first round. Fasten off.

Making up

Mark position of sleeves 23cm (9in) down from shoulder seams on back and front. Sew in sleeves between markers. Join side and sleeve seams.

Tweedy log basket

Keep your logs in line with this great basket, or use it for magazine storage by the fireside.

Thick tweed yarn and a textured basketweave pattern make an ideal sturdy fabric for this fireside basket with a circular base.

The Yarn

Sirdar Tweedie Chunky (approx. 100m/109 yards per 50g/1¾oz ball) contains 45% acrylic, 40% wool and 15% alpaca. This machine-washable yarn combines the good looks of wool with the practicalities of man-made fibres. There is a small range of natural shades and some bright colours, all with toning flecks of tweed.

GETTING STARTED

 Basic fabrics but making large size of basket requires patience.

Size:

45cm (17¾in) diameter at base x 138cm (54in) circumference at top x 32cm (12½in) high

How much yarn:

6 x 50g (1¾oz) balls of Sirdar Tweedie Chunky in colour A – Truffle (shade 281)
3 balls in colour B – Cedar (shade 285)
1 ball in colour C – Roasted Berry (shade 284)

Additional items:

1m (1⅛ yards) of 137cm (54in)-wide heavyweight fabric for lining
150cm (1⅝ yards) of 95cm (37½in)-wide heavyweight iron-on interfacing

Matching sewing and buttonhole threads

Hook:

5.50mm (UK 5) crochet hook

Tension:

13 sts and 11 rows measure 10cm (4in) square over patt on 5.50mm (UK 5) hook
IT IS ESSENTIAL TO WORK TO THE STATED TENSION TO ACHIEVE SUCCESS

What you have to do:

Work base in rounds of trebles, increasing to size. Continue in rounds, working sides in basketweave pattern and changing colours as directed. Work top edge and handles in double crochet. Machine sew an interfaced lining to strengthen basket.

Instructions

Abbreviations:

beg = beginning
ch = chain(s)
cm = centimetre(s)
cont = continue
dc = double crochet
foll = follows
inc = increases
patt = pattern
rep = repeat
rbtr = yrh, insert hook from back and from right to left around stem of next st and draw a loop through, complete tr in usual way
rftr = yrh, insert hook from front and right to left around stem of next st and draw a loop through, complete tr in usual way
RS = right side
ss = slip stitch
st(s) = stitch(es)
tr = treble(s)
WS = wrong side
yrh = yarn round hook

BASKET:
Base:
With 5.50mm (UK 5) hook and A, make 2ch.

1st round: 6dc into 2nd ch from hook, join with a ss into first dc. 6 sts.

2nd round: 3ch (counts as first tr), 1tr into st at base of ch, 2tr into each st to end, join with a ss into 3rd of 3ch. 12 sts.

3rd round: As 2nd round. 24 sts.

4th round: 3ch, miss first st, 2tr into next st, *1tr into next st, 2tr into next st, rep from * to end, join with a ss into 3rd of 3ch. 36 sts.

5th round: 3ch, miss first st, 1tr into next st, 2tr into next st, *1tr into each of next 2 sts, 2tr into next st, rep from * to end, join with a ss into 3rd of 3ch. 48 sts.

6th round: 3ch, miss first st, 1tr into each of next 2 sts, 2tr into next st, *1tr into each of next 3 sts, 2tr into next st, rep from * to end, join with a ss into 3rd of 3ch. 60 sts.

7th round: 3ch, miss first st, 1tr into each of next 3 sts, 2tr into next st, *1tr into each of next 4 sts, 2tr into next st, rep from * to end, join with a ss into 3rd of 3ch. 72 sts.

8th round: 3ch, miss first st, 1tr into each of next 4 sts, 2tr into next st, *1tr into each of next 5 sts, 2tr into next st, rep from * to end, join with a ss into 3rd of 3ch. 84 sts.

Cont in this way, working 1 more st between incs on every round, until there are 13 sts between incs and 180 sts in total. (Base should measure approximately 45cm (17¾in) in diameter.)

Sides:
Next round: 3ch, miss first st, 1tr into back loop only of each st to end, join with a ss into 3rd of 3ch.

Cont in basketweave patt as foll:

1st and 2nd rounds: 3ch, miss first st, 1rftr into each of next 2 sts, 1rbtr into each of next 3 sts, *1rftr into each of next 3 sts, 1rbtr into each of next 3 sts, rep from * to end, join with a ss into 3rd of 3ch.

3rd and 4th rounds: 3ch, miss first st, 1rbtr into each of next 2 sts, 1rftr into each of next 3 sts, *1rbtr into each of next 3 sts, 1rftr into each of next 3 sts, rep from * to end, join with a ss into 3rd of 3ch.

These 4 rounds form patt. Rep them until sides measure 20cm (8in) from beg, ending with a 2nd or 4th patt row. Change to B and cont in patt until sides measure 30cm (12in) from beg, ending with a 2nd or 4th patt row. Change to C and work 2 more rounds in patt. Do not fasten off.

Shape handles:
Place basket flat and mark centre of top edge on both sides. Count out 15 sts at either side of centre and insert markers for handles.

First handle: 1ch (counts as first dc), 1dc into each st along top edge of basket to first marker, **36ch, miss 30 sts of top edge of basket, ss into next st, turn.

1st row: 1dc into same st as ss, working along inner edge of handle work 1dc into each ch to end, ss in next free st on top edge between handle, turn.

2nd row: 1dc in same st as ss, 1dc into each st of handle, ss into next free st on top edge between handle, turn.

3rd row: 1dc in same st as ss, 1dc into each st of handle, 1dc into each st on top edge between handle, ss across row ends of handle**, 1dc into each st along top edge of basket to first marker for second handle.

Second handle: Work as 1st handle from ** to **, 1dc into each st along top edge of basket to beg of round, ss in 1ch. Fasten off.

 ## Making up

From both lining fabric and interfacing, cut a 48cm (19in)-diameter circle for the base and two strips, each 31 × 73cm (12¼ × 28¾in), for the sides. Trim away 1.5cm (⅝in) all around interfacing circle and strips, then iron onto WS of lining fabric, centering each piece to leave 1.5cm (⅝in) seam allowance around outer edges. With RS facing and taking a 1.5cm (⅝in) seam allowance, join short ends of strips to form an open-ended circular piece. Turn 1.5cm (⅝in) to WS along one open edge and

secure with two parallel lines of machine-stitching 5mm (¼in) apart. With RS facing and taking 1.5cm (⅝in) seam allowance, pin and tack other open edge to base, easing in any fullness. Machine stitch, remove tacking and zigzag raw edges together.

Insert lining into basket with WS of lining to WS of basket. Pin top edge of lining just below top edge of basket and slip stitch securely in place with buttonhole thread.

Index

Acknowledgements

Managing Editor: Clare Churly
Editors: Lesley Malkin and Eleanor van Zandt
Senior Art Editor: Juliette Norsworthy
Designer: Janis Utton
Production Controller: Allison Gonsalves